STANDOUT

StandOut

*The Groundbreaking New Strengths Assessment
from the Leader of the **Strengths Revolution***

MARCUS BUCKINGHAM

THOMAS NELSON
Since 1798

NASHVILLE   DALLAS   MEXICO CITY   RIO DE JANEIRO

Published in Nashville, Tennessee, by Thomas Nelson. Thomas Nelson is a registered trademark of Thomas Nelson, Inc.

Page design by Mandi Cofer.

Thomas Nelson, Inc., titles may be purchased in bulk for educational, business, fund-raising, or sales promotional use. For information, please e-mail SpecialMarkets@ThomasNelson.com.

ISBN 978-0-8499-4888-6 (IE)

Library of Congress Cataloging-in-Publication Data

Buckingham, Marcus.
  StandOut : the groundbreaking new strengths assessment from the leader of the strengths revolution / Marcus Buckingham.
    p. cm.
  ISBN 978-1-4002-0237-9 (alk. paper)
1. Creative ability in business. 2. Employee motivation. 3. Executive ability. 4. Leadership. I. Title. II. Title: Stand out.
  HD53.B83 2011
  658.4'063--dc22

                              2011009101

                 Printed in the United States of America

                   14 15 16 QG 18 17 16 15

To the entire Buckingham family,
who made the best of me;
and
To my extended TMBC family,
who made the best of StandOut.

Contents

CHAPTER 1

"Whistles for Everyone!"

How to Accelerate Innovation

The StandOut strengths assessment is an innovation delivery system. We designed it to reveal your edge, and then feed you practical innovations, tips, and techniques that you can use to sharpen this edge and win at work.

We all revere innovation. It is the mystical driver of progress, the secret sauce, the touchstone we reach for whenever our backs are against the wall. Our managers, our leaders, even our president cajole us to outthink, outsmart, "out-innovate" the competition. In these accelerated times, only innovation will keep us relevant, only innovation will allow us to keep thriving, only innovation can get us ahead and keep us there.

And when we say this, what do we mean by *innovation*? Usually we mean *invention* and we point back to that Golden Age of invention, the *Apollo* years, when anything was possible, when failure was not an option, when necessity created Teflon and freeze-dried food, the Stairmaster and digital photography, the technology inside every kidney-dialysis machine and the materials for your running shoes, solar panels and better golf balls, and, of course, ARPANet, the forerunner to the Internet. Heady times. No wonder our leaders hark back to them.

For most of us, though, innovation is a little less dramatic. We aren't looking to invent the Internet. We just want a better technique, a better way of doing things. We are tantalized by the notion that someone in our field has devised a method or figured out a shortcut, the "control-C" or "control-P," of our job, something that if we could just find and replicate, we would be able to take a giant leap forward in our performance and in our career.

And our employers are possessed by the very same notion. Every organization is on a near-constant search for "best practice." They convene conferences of top performers, pick their brains for the precious few actions, and then capture what they hear in online "knowledge centers," in videos, or in the course books of their corporate university. Though it is not always stated explicitly, the vision driving all of this activity is that innovation can be harvested and that, once harvested, it can be deployed at scale. Find a few key innovations, so the thinking goes, and we'll spread them to the many.

And occasionally, very occasionally, it does work this way. In the early twentieth century, Dr. Henry Plummer of the Mayo Clinic was experimenting with the use of X-rays for medical purposes. Although he and his team of clinicians had all the right equipment, they kept getting blurred images of their patients. Dr. Plummer and his team tried telling the patients "Don't move." But they moved anyway. Then they phrased it more positively. "Hold still," they said. But the patients couldn't hold still long enough to avoid blurring the picture, particularly when their head or torso were being X-rayed. Undaunted, Dr. Plummer worked on the problem until finally he happened upon the one phrase that magically transformed his patients into statues. This phrase proved so effective that still, today, when you are waiting in the radiology room for your X-ray, the nurse will turn to you and say: "Please hold your breath."

He had found one key innovation, and in the intervening century it has been deployed at massive scale.

Annoyingly, Dr. Plummer's experience is the exception. It is very rare to discover a best practice that is transferable person to person at such scale, with no lessening of its effectiveness. Normally what happens is this: An enterprising employee will come up with a new way of doing things. This new practice will spring from within her as an irrepressible manifestation of her personality. It will be authentic and natural, and she will use it to outperform her colleagues. This success will bring her to the attention of her superiors, who will interview her to discover her secret. Her new practice will be elevated up the corporate ladder, vetted by Operations, Human Resources, Training, Communications, and Legal, until eventually, stripped of its unique characteristics and the person who made them, it will be introduced to the rest of the "field," where it will end its life as just another corporate program, smoothed out and lifeless, inauthentic for everyone else and ineffective for the company.

A few years ago in a study of top-performing managers for Best Buy, I had the chance to interview Ralph Gonzalez. Ralph had successfully transformed one of Best Buy's lowest-performing stores into a repeat award winner. On virtually every metric, from revenues to profitability to employee engagement to "shrink," he had taken his team from the bottom 10 percent to the top. What had he done, I asked him, to effect such a dramatic transformation?

He told me that he had played on his likeness to a young

Fidel Castro, that he had called his store "La Revolucion," that he had posted a "Declaracion de Revolucion" in the break room, that he had made the supervisors wear army fatigues, and then, as I was scribbling all this down, he told me about the whistle.

It was a brilliant innovation. Since initially his store was at the bottom of every district performance table, he wanted to give his people a way to celebrate that excellence was indeed happening in his store, and that it was happening all the time. So he gave everyone a whistle and told them to blow the whistle whenever they saw anyone do anything good. It didn't matter if the person they saw was their superior or was working over in another department; if they saw somebody go above and beyond, they were to blow the whistle.

"Didn't it make the store incredibly loud?" I asked.

"Sure," he replied, with a glinty Castro grin. "But it energized the store. It energized me. Heck, it even energized the customers. They loved it."

I was so taken with this innovation I wrote about it in *Now, Discover Your Strengths*. What I didn't describe is what happened next. Having been shared at a number of company gatherings, the "whistle story" started to take on a life of its own. All of a sudden it began cropping up in different districts and regions around the country. "Whistles for everyone!" There was even talk of devising a system to properly implement the whistle inside a store. Managers would have green whistles, supervisors white, and frontline blue-shirts regular silver whistles. Here are the twelve conditions when whistles can be blown—and here are the twenty conditions when the whistle must *not* be blown, no exceptions. What had begun as a vibrant expression of a particular person's personality was fast mutating into a "Standard Operating Procedure."

Fortunately, some wise Best Buy executives, realizing that this innovation was almost entirely dependent on the presence of Ralph himself, stepped in and killed the mutation before it could spread.

Ralph's whistle reveals both the problem and the power of innovation: namely that innovation is a practice, not an idea. Invention is an idea, a novel idea, and, like all ideas, a novel idea is easily transferable from person to person—introduce one person to the concept of personal liberty, he tells another, she passes it on to a third, and, like a benign infection, pretty soon the whole country is swept up in the mission to secure personal liberty for all.

Innovation is "novelty that can be applied." This means that there is a person involved, someone actually doing the doing, a Ralph. An innovation is transferable only if the person you are delivering the innovation to has the same strengths as the person who created it in the first place. What is effective and authentic in the hands of one person looks forced, fake, and foolish in the hands of another.

We see this most glaringly on the world stage. The equivalent of the "whistle" for U.S. presidents is the military photo-shoot. If a president or a presidential candidate can secure an appearance with the military, the visual image reads as powerful and authoritative. But, of course, this "best practice" depends heavily on who the practitioner is. Have President George W. Bush land on an aircraft carrier and emerge in full flight gear, and he looks authentically presidential (despite the subsequent overreach of the "Mission Accomplished" banner behind him). Have Michael Dukakis poke his head out of the turret of a tank and he looks, well, silly.

But it also applies to any best practice, in any position or endeavor. Recently my company, TMBC, undertook a best practice study of the top 10 percent of Hilton's Focused Service brands' general managers—Hampton Inn, Hilton Garden Inn, Homewood Suites, and Home 2. Since Hampton Inn was just voted the best franchisor in the country by *Entrepreneur* magazine—ahead of the likes of McDonald's and Subway—and since Hilton Garden Inn and Homewood Suites are multi-year J.D. Power award winners, we knew that, in targeting their top 10 percent, we were interviewing some truly excellent performers.

Although during the interviews it became apparent that they shared similar approaches to some things, it was their differences that were most striking. Diana runs the Hampton Inn and Suites in Ephrata, Pennsylvania. Vivacious and excitable (and chatty—my forty-five minute interview was still going strong at an hour and fifteen) Diana has been a perennial award winner since she opened the hotel five years ago.

"What's your secret?" I asked her. "I mean, if there were a few things you would tell every manager they should do if they are to succeed, what would they be?"

"First, get a mascot," she replied.

"A mascot?"

"Yep. A mascot. Every hotel should have one. It gives the employees and the guests something to rally around. A personality. A purpose."

"What's yours?"

"The turtle."

"What? Why?"

"Because, like the turtle, we won't make any progress unless we stick our necks out. The turtle is so cool. We have them everywhere here. If you could see my office, it's full of plush turtles. When you win employee of the month, you are the 'turtle of the month.' Our regular guests get little toy turtles to take back to their kids. It's an awesome thing. I've been telling every hotel manager I run into that they should get a mascot. In fact, I've just heard that another Hampton down the way are now 'the bees' because, you know, they don't get anything done unless they work together."

So I talked to Diana for an hour or so about her turtles and a part of me thought, *Really, turtles?* and another part thought, *Well, if it works, it works*, and then I hung up the phone and called Tim. Tim runs the Hilton Garden Inn in Times Square, and he's another superstar. But he's no Diana. He's quieter, more cerebral.

"A practice I would share with others?" he repeated my question. A long pause. "Well, I don't really have one. I think my people have all the answers. That's the way I run my hotel. I tell my people that they are closer to the guest than I am, that they know this hotel better than I do, and that, whether it's a guest issue or something to do with the property, they'll know the answers."

I kept probing. "That's an interesting perspective, Tim, but can you think of any ways that you put this perspective into practice? Anything, anything at all?"

"Well, there's our lending library, of course."

"Excuse me?"

"We have a lending library. I decided that if my people were going to have all the answers, then we needed to be a learning hotel, and what better way to symbolize learning than to ask every employee to bring in one book per month and we would set up a lending library. It doesn't matter if it's a fiction book, nonfiction, or even a kids' book, we still want you to bring it in. All of you have something to teach us, something we can learn from. So bring in a book, borrow other people's books, and we'll all learn together."

These are but two innovations from two superstar managers. With my prodding Tim told me about many more. So did Diana. So did they all. And yet, very few of these innovations would have been transferable from one person to another, even though they all came from top performers doing the same job, at the same level, in the same organization. Tell Tim that he absolutely must have a mascot for his hotel and what would he have picked? The bookworm? The owl? Most likely he would have picked nothing and procrastinated in hopes that the new corporate "mascot" program would soon wither away. Tell Diana to start a lending library and, while she might rouse herself to put her own spin on it, most likely she would dismiss it. Not exciting enough. Not her thing.

Two engineers in one of the social media giants offer us another example. David writes code. And he's a certain kind of coder. He is a "massager." Give him ten or more hours of uninterrupted coding time and he will massage the code, working and reworking it until it is so efficient and so elegant that others will read the code just to admire it. He refuses to come to the office. He works from home, alone with his dog, Bit. His secret sauce, he said, is extended solitude.

Not so for Luke. He's another exemplary engineer at the same company, but he's not a massager. He's a "salvager." He takes one person's failed coding experiment, reconstructs what the person was trying to do, combines it with another person's experiment, and creates something neither had initially intended. His genius—although he'd be uncomfortable with that label—is asking probing questions without making the original designer defensive, a practice he calls the "Guessing Game."

During his company's once a month code-a-thons—where all engineers who want to can stay up the entire night coding, drinking, munching, and then shipping code the next morning—he can be found moving from one engineer to another, playfully guessing where they were intending to take the code, and throwing in a couple of intriguing "guesses" of his own. These guesses, in turn, prompt new ideas from the original designers, which he then pieces together into a workable program.

Tell Luke to spend ten hours of solitude a day and he'd see it as a punishment, not a best practice.

Try to teach David the mechanics of the "Guessing Game" and he'd dismiss you as a know-nothing crank.

We have studied the country's best high school principals, the best affiliate leaders of Habitat for Humanity, the best emergency room nurses, and the best pharmaceutical sales reps, and whenever we interview excellent performers in the same position, we find this same phenomenon—extraordinary results achieved in radically different ways. Yes, there may be some similar practices among those who excel in a certain position (see chapter 5, the Technical Summary, for a few examples), but no, for any position, there is no "perfect" profile; there are only perfect practices that fit your particular profile.

So, what your organization wants are not the few innovations that can be scaled to the many. Instead, what your organization wants are *many* practical innovations and a way to deliver these innovations to those *few* people who share the strengths of the person who dreamed up each one of them.

And this is what you want too. Instead of top-down initiatives that feel awkward and inauthentic, you want to be introduced to practical innovations that you might well have thought of . . . but haven't yet; techniques that, when you try them out, feel as though you've done them before. You want to accelerate your creativity and yet still retain your authenticity.

This is why we built the StandOut strengths assessment. Over the last decade, we captured many hundreds of techniques, practices, and insights—for leaders, for managers, for client service positions, for sales, for individual contributors of all kinds—and we loaded them into the back end of the assessment. Once you've completed it, you will receive only those practices that fit your particular strengths. You will receive the best practical innovations, broadcast on the You channel.

Facebook, Netflix, Slacker, and StandOut

By filtering content to fit you, StandOut is mirroring in the field of best practices what we see happening in other fields.

For example, in the entertainment world content used to be gathered in one central place and then pushed out to you, no matter who you were. ESPN pushed out sports programming. CBS broadcast comforting sitcoms. The History Channel collected, edited, and distributed newsreel footage of World War II.

To get what you wanted you had to sort through all five hundred channels and pinpoint the one or two shows that truly matched your tastes.

To some extent this still works, but with such a proliferation of centralized content, the burden is on *you* to sift through it all.

Today's most successful companies are working to relieve you of that burden. And at the same time matching you with content more accurately than you could yourself. Facebook is now an advertising powerhouse not because it has a centralized stock of better ads, but because the first question it asks is "Who are you?" and only then, guided by its understanding of your unique profile of likes and dislikes, does it deliver ads that "fit" your profile.

Netflix does the same. Before you can stream a movie, it gives you a "movie quiz." It presents you with a series of movies, asks you if you've seen them and how you'd rate each one, and then based on the results of your quiz, it suggests only those movies that match your past preferences.

Pandora radio and Slacker radio do much the same thing with music. Both of these services, in slightly different ways, "listen" to what you choose to listen to and then play you only music that is similar to your inferred musical tastes.

In each of these cases, what's centralized is an understanding of you. This understanding of you, this algorithm-derived avatar, then becomes the filter through which the content is delivered. The algorithm isn't perfect—sometimes you find yourself listening to Lady Gaga when what you really wanted was a Lady Antebellum song—but its focus is. Its focus is you:

your habits, your preferences, your movie favorites, your musical quirks, and, in the case of StandOut, your strengths.

Within your job alone there are hundreds of possible practices and innovations; across all the different people who do your job there are uncountable combinations of strengths and weaknesses. What you (and your manager) need is a Rosetta stone to make sense of this complexity and match the right innovations to the right strengths. StandOut is your Rosetta stone.

CHAPTER 2

The New StandOut Strengths Assessment

What It Measures, How It Works, and How to Take It

The StandOut assessment measures you on nine strength Roles and reveals your top two. These two strength Roles are where you will make your greatest contribution. They are your *edge*—where you will have a natural advantage over everyone else. And they are your *multiplier*—you will most quickly learn and improve upon any innovations, techniques, or best practices that complement these two Roles.

With each of your top two Roles you will receive this advice:

- *Phrases to describe your edge*—As most of us do, you probably struggle to find the right words to capture what makes you stand out. You are either too vague: "I like challenge." Or you overcompensate, and lurch into flagrant self-promotion: "I was in President's Club five years straight." You need suggestions for how to be specific about your strengths, without being a braggadocio.

- *How to make an immediate impact*—You've just joined your new team or stepped into a new position within your current team. You want to make an immediate and solid first impression. How can you do this purposefully? What are your quickest wins? Where will you surprise people with the speed of your uptake?

- *How to take your performance to the next level*—So you're now an established member of the team. How can you elevate your performance and become a lynchpin, the proverbial franchise player, the one whom they tell stories about at company gatherings, the one whom the biggest and best clients request?

- *What to watch out for*—You can never have too much of a strength, but you can misdirect it or channel it poorly. What are the pitfalls to which you are susceptible and which could you, with forethought, avoid?

When you receive your results, read the practices and techniques for each Role and then click on the "Combine My Top 2 Roles" button and you will discover what you can do to maximize your distinct combination. Here you will find:

- *Which careers fit your strengths combination*—Although we have seen each strength Role combination in every career we have studied, we have also been able to map particular combinations to particular jobs and responsibilities. Here you will find which responsibilities are the closest fits for your specific strengths combination.

- *How you can win as a leader*—All great leaders rally people to a better future, but each does it differently. Since authenticity is the currency of effective leadership, you need to know your natural leadership edge. How can you make your people believe that you believe in a better future for your organization? How can you genuinely convey your optimism without being a Pollyanna? How can you transform your people's uncertainty into genuine confidence, when, truth be told, you have uncertainties of your own? Which practices will accelerate your growth and effectiveness as a leader?

- *How you can win as a manager*—All great managers turn one person's talent into performance, but your way of doing this will depend on your unique combination of strength Roles. So, what is your best way of setting clear expectations for people, for rewarding people, for engaging them, for challenging them?

- *How you can win in sales*—We are all salespeople. We all have someone whom we are trying to persuade, someone whose commitment we seek. How do you convince? When do you come across as persuasive? If you ever needed to make your case compelling, how would you do it? How do you move others to action?

- *How you can win in client service*—All of us have clients; some are external, some internal, but all of us are in the service of someone. The chief responsibility of client service is to build a relationship with the client that extends beyond price. What is your way of doing this? How can you give your clients certainty? How can you establish trust with them? How can they learn from you?

What the StandOut Strengths Assessment Measures

Spend twenty years building and analyzing tests that measure people's themes of talent, and over time it becomes apparent that, no matter how thinly you slice each aspect of each theme, certain themes do wind up clustering into patterns.

For example, it is entirely possible to design an assessment that draws a distinction between themes such as Significance, Self-Assurance, Achievement Drive, and Assertiveness and then measures them separately—Dr. Don Clifton and I did this with StrengthsFinder. What we now know, however, is that these four themes correlate closely with one another. In statistical parlance a set of highly correlated themes is called a "factor," but in the real world they combine to create a certain "personality," a certain way of engaging with the world. In the case of these four themes, we know this personality well. It is the person who wants others to come around to his way of thinking, who enjoys persuading, outsmarting, or outwitting people, and who can even, on occasion, come across as aggressive. In the language of StandOut, this person is an Influencer.

Similarly, a combination of the themes Strategic Thinking, Optimism, Impatience, and Ambiguity Tolerance creates another kind of person. This is the person who is at her best charging into the future, believing in every fiber that the world is a friendly place, that setbacks are opportunities in disguise, and that the best way to find out what is around the next corner is to walk around the corner and see for herself. In the language of StandOut, this person is a Pioneer and she's different from the rest of us: the uncertainty that unnerves us, thrills her.

To create the StandOut strengths assessment, we combed through all the many hundreds of themes that are possible to measure, and identified the most common and powerful theme combinations. Of course, the number of ways to measure the fine shadings of human uniqueness is infinite; however, the number of powerful theme combinations is not. We found nine. We call them "Strength Roles."

 Advisor

You are a practical, concrete thinker who is at your most powerful when reacting to and solving other people's problems.

 Connector

You are a catalyst. Your power lies in your craving to bring two people or ideas together to make something bigger and better than it is now.

 Creator

You make sense of the world—pulling it apart, seeing a better configuration, and creating it.

 Equalizer

You are a levelheaded person whose power comes from keeping the world in balance, ethically and practically.

 Influencer

You engage people directly and convince them to act. Your power is your persuasion.

Pioneer

You see the world as a friendly place where around every corner good things will happen. Your power comes from your optimism in the face of uncertainty.

Provider

You sense other people's feelings, and you feel compelled to recognize these feelings, give them a voice, and act on them.

Stimulator

You are the host of other people's emotions. You feel responsible for them, for turning them around, for elevating them.

Teacher

You are thrilled by the potential you see in each person. Your power comes from learning how to unleash it.

Inside the Black Box: How the StandOut Strengths Assessment Works

If you've always wondered how you can figure out a person's distinctive edge—even though he knows that this is precisely what you are trying to do, and even though he may not know it himself—this section will open the black box a crack.

As I described in *Now, Discover Your Strengths*, your real-world performance for any given day is the sum of all the moment-by-moment choices you make. If someone challenged you during the day, what did you do? If you realized that you'd let someone down, what was your first reaction? When a friend who really needed you distracted you from the task at hand, which one got your immediate attention?

Of course, the simple answer to all these questions is "it depends." On who was challenging you, on whom you let down. On what you were doing when the friend called.

And yet your reactions were not entirely random. They didn't depend exclusively on the other person, the situation, or the task at hand. Many of them depended mostly on you. Are you the sort of person who generally responds positively to being challenged, or who doesn't; who has a gut-level negative reaction to letting someone down, or who can find a way to rationalize it; who will never allow herself to be distracted from the task at hand, no matter how close and needy the friend, or who feels the friend's need so acutely it's almost a physical pain? There are patterns here, patterns in you. And the most dominant—the most frequently recurring patterns—are the source of your strengths.

How can we measure them?

Ten years ago, in StrengthsFinder, we chose to give you self-descriptors, such as "Are you a teacher or are you a coach?" The benefit of this method is that it is simple. You are given two choices, you make one, you click the button, and you move on to the next choice.

This was the best method of its time, but it does have a downside: because the self-descriptors are spelled out, it is obvious to the test taker what each pair is trying to measure. This means that the results can be thrown off, either if the test taker is utterly clueless about who she is, or if she is actively trying to skew the test to produce a desired result.

Over the last decade we've learned that the best way to combat this downside is to construct a different kind of assessment; one built not around straightforward self-descriptors but around something a little, well, sneakier.

In StandOut we mirror the stimulus-response of the real world by presenting you with a stimulus—in most cases, a slightly stressful situation—and then offering you a set of possible responses. Then we do the following three things. First, we put you under a timer—forty-five seconds—so that you don't have the chance to overthink your response. Second, all of the choices appear equally "good." For example, we might ask you: *A new teammate comes to you really excited about an idea she is sure will help your team excel. What do you do?*

And then, just as you're thinking this over, up come these four choices:

A. Run her idea by the rest of the team to see what they think.
B. Ask her some challenging questions to see if she's thought it all the way through.
C. Highlight what's great about the idea and help her build on this.
D. Try it out and see if it works.

Any one of these could be defended as a sensible thing to do. Yes, you may disagree with one or two of them, but none of them are obviously correct.

Third, we embed in each choice specific "trigger words." A trigger word is a word that we know stimulates a certain kind of person's reticular activating center and, whether she is conscious of it or not, captures her attention. For example, we know that when you want to measure competitiveness, the word *score* is a trigger word. Give a person four possible responses and include in one the word *score*, and, even if the word *score* is not a central part of the response, competitors will still pick it. Thinking back, they won't necessarily be able to tell you why they chose it, but they will choose it nonetheless.

If you want to assess empathy, we know that the word *cry* is a trigger word—empathetic people self-report that they cry with and cry for others more often than the rest of us do. Slip the word *cry* into a scenario and although the number of people who pick that response will fall—perhaps because many of us think that crying isn't what grown-ups do—those few who do pick it will have talent for feeling the emotions of others. In other words, they will be empathetic.

I won't give you any other examples because, frankly, StandOut is littered with them—virtually every choice to every scenario is constructed around a trigger word. Don't try to spot them, just read the scenarios and let your reticular activating center do what it was designed to do.

The bottom line is this: when you take StandOut it is irrelevant whether you know yourself well or not, or whether you are trying to skew the test toward a certain result, or even whether you think to yourself that you wouldn't pick any of the four responses. You'll simply see the scenario, read the responses, and then, guided by your conscious mind or your unconscious triggers, you'll make your choice.

And don't worry—if you miss a question, or if in retrospect

you are unhappy with your choice, we will give you eleven more chances to make a choice that "hits" each of the nine strength Roles.

You'll then reach the end of StandOut, the algorithm will do its calculating, choice totals will be tallied, outliers removed, patterns found, and finally your results will appear. These results may surprise you, or they may confirm what you have long believed about yourself. Either way, remember that *StandOut* does not reveal how well you know yourself—after all, we haven't asked you to rate yourself on a list of qualities. Instead, because *StandOut* measures which way you instinctively react to the scenarios, your results reveal how you come across to others. When you join a team, *this* is what your teammates feel from you. When you engage a client, *this* is the impact you have on her. When you lead a team forward, *this* is the sense they make of you. So, when you read your results, keep your mind open to the possibility that, no matter how you see yourself, *this* is how others see you.

A Sharper Focus: How StandOut Builds on StrengthsFinder

Back in 1999 we designed StrengthsFinder to give you positive language to describe yourself. If that sounds a little touchy-feely, remember that before StrengthsFinder psychology was so preoccupied with pathology that although we had a thousand-page bible of psychological disease—the *Diagnostic and Statistical Manual of Mental Disorders* (DSM)—we had no common language to describe what was *right* about you.

To help redress this imbalance, Dr. Don Clifton and I

crafted the questions and themes of StrengthsFinder and published them in *Now, Discover Your Strengths*. (To be precise, Don devised the questions and I wrote the themes.) The purpose of this assessment was to be descriptive and affirming. We wanted to give you a way to describe the best of you and to make you feel good about your style.

I'm pleased to say that it has proven so popular that, to date, more than five million people have taken it.

The challenge, of course, is that once you have a positive language to describe yourself, what do you do with it? What careers should you pursue? What techniques should you call upon to capitalize on your strengths and outperform your competitors? What should you share with your manager to help him or her help you do your best work?

I believe that if we had stayed together, Don and I would have continued to refine StrengthsFinder so that it could answer these questions. But we couldn't stay together and do this work. Don passed away in 2003, and after his death I left Gallup to focus less on measurement—Gallup's forte—and more on what could be done to increase the very things we were measuring—employee engagement, strengths, performance.

As part of this focus on action over measurement, our team—I worked with Dr. Courtney McCashland on the scenarios, with Tracy Hutton and Charlotte Jordan on the action items, and Jaqai Mickelsen on design—built a strengths assessment to answer these questions. We wanted an assessment that would reveal your edge and give you practical innovations to help you sharpen this edge. Where StrengthsFinder was descriptive and affirming, we wanted StandOut to be *prescriptive* and *innovating*.

The Manager's Team Report

We also wanted to develop a tool that would show managers specifically what they could do to focus, reward, and challenge each direct report. StrengthsFinder was complicated enough— it measured you on thirty-four themes and displayed your top five—that managers were often overwhelmed. Each team member would feel affirmed, but the manager would frequently be left with a more complex world remembering the top five results for each team member and ten to fifteen actions for each role.

So, whereas StrengthsFinder teased you apart to reveal the complexities of your style, StandOut puts you back together and highlights where you have a competitive advantage. Your manager needs to know this, simply and clearly. And then he or she needs a "cheat sheet" filled with ideas, actions, tips, and techniques to help you make the most of it. The optional Manager's Team Report on the StandOut website serves up this "cheat sheet."

Okay. Time to Take StandOut.

Go to standout.tmbc.com, input your key, and the assessment will begin. You'll hear me asking you each question—we added this feature to encourage in you a more immediate response— the "gate" will open, and your four options will appear. Read them quickly—the timer in the center of the screen will show you how much time you have left—and then allow your instincts to guide your choice. You have fifteen minutes. Good luck. I hope you enjoy it.

CHAPTER 3

The Nine Strengths Roles

ADVISOR

CONNECTOR

CREATOR

EQUALIZER

INFLUENCER

PIONEER

PROVIDER

STIMULATOR

TEACHER

ADVISOR

The Definition

You begin by asking, *"What is the best thing to do?"* and your thrill comes from knowing that you are the person others turn to for the answer. You don't necessarily want to be the person who actually makes the changes happen. Rather, being valued by others for your insight and your judgment is what excites you. Since you love to be the expert, you are constantly on the lookout for information that will help people make better decisions. When you look out at the world, you pay attention to fine shadings of detail because these details will ensure that you give better advice. You know that the best advice is never general, but rather is tailored to the unique characteristics of the person's situation.

You can be demanding and opinionated, but above all you are discriminating: "good enough" is never good enough for you. There is always a better way, a better arrangement, a better solution, and you come alive when you are called upon to find it. And when you do, you don't question your decision. The reason people seek your advice is precisely because you are so assured, so confident in your intuition. Instinctively you know this, and you're proud of it.

You, at Your Most Powerful

- You are connected to someone else through the advice you are giving. In fact, your advice is how you connect with other people.

- You are a practical, concrete thinker. You think in terms of "steps" and "modules." The language you use is: "Here are the steps I recommend." "Write down these tips." "Here are the materials I've developed."

- You are a problem solver. You are not fazed by complex situations, because when faced with a challenge, you break it down into its component parts. You are a sequential thinker, someone who excels at "delayering" problems, "unstacking" them.

- You ask lots of questions because the answer can be found in the details of the situation. You are intrigued by the detail of other people's plans, problems, lives. You are not voyeuristic—voyeurism is too passive. But you can be nosy.

- You like distinctions between two things that seem quite similar. These distinctions help you know how to choose which path to take—"Take this one, not that one."

- You are very respectful of other experts. Experts are able to see fine distinctions, and you respect distinctions.

- You are not intrigued by the future or by novelty merely for the sake of it (unless your second strengths Role is Pioneer). Nonetheless you can be innovative, because your question is always "What is the best thing to do?" or "What will work?" and sometimes this leads you to solutions that haven't been tried before. As such, you are not tied down to existing ways of doing things.

- When you write something you feel compelled to think about the person on the receiving end of what you are writing. You think not in terms of "Here is an idea I'd like to present," but rather in terms of "*You* should do this . . ." You like being seen as the expert. You like being needed in this way. When people say, "You have such great insight. You give me such a useful perspective on my situation," this is the highest of praise.

- You are never stumped. You always think you have a solution, a way forward. Other people are drawn to you because they see someone (in you) who is supremely capable.

- Your "time suck" is people asking you out for lunch all the time. "What should I do about this and that?" they ask, and you can't help yourself. Off you go to lunch. Consequently you run the risk of not taking a stand for yourself. You are so busy offering advice that you don't stop to take your own. You can be a pushover when you are cornered and asked, "Please tell me what to do!" Your time is not your own.

How to Describe Yourself (in Interviews, Performance Reviews)

- "People say I have a lot of common sense. They come to me whenever they want advice on the best thing to do."

- "I'm at my best when pulling apart complex problems and figuring out what's actually going on."

- "I love helping people sort through what's confusing them to get to the best course of action."

- "I'm a very practical thinker. The most important thing for me is always to ask, 'What is really going to work?' "

- "I'm not tied to a set way of doing things. So long as what we are about to do is really going to work, I have no problem breaking new ground."

- "I've found that I'm the teammate people turn to when they're stuck. I help them get unstuck."

- "I love solutions . . . and always feel I can come up with them, no matter how much of a mess we are in. I can always find a practical way forward."

How to Make an Immediate Impact

- You are the rare person who is energized by other people's problems. So, to make an immediate impact, **seek out some of the toughest problems that either your team or your client is facing and set about tackling them**. Problem solving is draining for most people, but not you. This sets you apart.

- The thornier and more complicated the problem, the better. One of your best qualities is your ability to break a complex problem down into its component parts. So ask lots of practical questions, push aside people's generalizations, and get to the facts. **Show your colleagues how to "unpack" a complex problem and solve each part separately**. They'll be grateful. And you'll be at your best.

- **Put yourself in the middle of pivotal, intense moments**. When other people are stumped and at their wits' end, you are at your best. You think more clearly, project more confidence, act with more certainty. Whether your colleagues let on or not, they crave—and need—your confidence in high-pressure situations.

- **Seize any chance you get to explain how things work**— with a customer, at a staff meeting, or at a company gathering. You are at your most powerful and charismatic when breaking a process or situation down so that other people can see what is really going on.

- Every team leader has a couple of processes he knows aren't good but which are "good enough." They annoy him, but he tolerates them because the team is busy—"good enough" will have to do for right now. You can help him. **Take one of these "good enoughs" as a side project and come up with a practical solution for making it work right**. He may not understand exactly how you did it, but he will see this as "initiative."

- Since you feel truly alive only when you are tackling a difficult challenge, you can find yourself becoming bored when things are ticking along nicely. You may wish you weren't this way—"Why can't I be happy with business-as-usual?"—but you are. To avoid boredom either **carve your role into one where you are being paid to react and respond to problems** or, failing that, embrace the concept of *kaizen*—"continuous improvement"—and focus on those parts of your world that are not yet as effective as they could be.

How to Take Your Performance to the Next Level

- An Advisor always needs people to advise. Analysis is fine, and can be fun, but the day you discover that you have no direct audience for your conclusions—sitting by yourself, analyzing for the sake of it—will be a very bad day for you. **Make sure you are always being paid to offer your conclusions to someone.** You need this "someone," this "someone with a dilemma," to prove to yourself that you are valuable. And smart.

- You are the kind of person who respects experts. Why? Because experts have studied their subjects deeply and can pinpoint which details make the difference, which distinctions really matter. You are wired to appreciate this kind of inquiry. **So ally yourself with a couple of carefully chosen experts in your field.** Hang out with them. Read their articles or books. Volunteer to support them in their next big project. Their practical wisdom will intrigue and inspire you.

- **Become a credentialed expert yourself.** Choose your discipline and then build your career around deepening your expertise in this discipline. Pursue all the professional and academic qualifications available within this discipline. Your long-term career success hinges on your credibility and, like it or not—actually, you do like it—these sorts of qualifications, publicly displayed, give you an extra boost of credibility.

- These qualifications will also give you detail and, as an Advisor, **you do wonders with detail**. With some people detail disappears inside their heads into ever more convoluted theories and concepts. Not so with you. Your command of detail gets displayed for us all to see. The deeper you investigate a subject, the more fine-tuned and subtle your distinctions become. Since your mind instinctively uses distinctions to clarify other people's problems—"What's unique about your situation is X, and that's precisely why you should do Y, and not Z"—your deepening expertise makes your advice so much more insightful and effective.

- You are at your best when you can see the people on the receiving end of your strength as an Advisor. So, as your career progresses **seek out more demanding audiences**. "More demanding" might mean "wider"—can you publish your insights in blogs, articles, or even books? It might mean a more discriminating audience—a group of your peers, perhaps, or your most valuable customers. It might mean a higher profile audience—the "C" suite or the highest levels of government. Or it might mean a higher stakes audience—the launching of a business, children at risk, or national security.

- You will always be at your best when the route ahead is unclear and someone needs to come in, assess all the facts available, and make a decision. **Start-ups fit this description nicely**. Your career could very well be a series of start-ups that require your particular gift for pragmatic decision making.

What to Watch Out For

- Don't come across as a know-it-all. Some Advisors fall prey to this caricature because they not only seem to have all the answers, they also appear so certain of their answers. To avoid this, before you launch into what you know is the right answer, **discipline yourself to ask plenty of questions**. Even if after asking your very first question, you think that you know the best course of action, keep asking questions two through ten. For the other person to accept your advice, she will need to feel that you have truly heard all there is to hear about her situation.

- You are not at your best running existing operations. It bores you. You are a turnaround person, a start-up person. **You are not a builder**. So don't allow yourself to be cast as one.

- **Don't let yourself get promoted too far away from the action**. And for you action means the drama, the variety, and the urgent need of other people's challenges. Responding to these challenges is the stuff of life. No matter how much money is being offered to you, no matter how enticing your new title will be, never convince yourself that it can be delegated. With you, it can't.

- Don't become a shoeless cobbler. If you're not careful you'll get so drawn to the challenge of solving other people's problems you will neglect your own and allow them to pile up. You may not notice this happening—other people's predicaments can be so intriguing—but gradually the pressure will build, until one day you wake up and realize that you are bent double beneath the weight of your own unresolved issues. At that point your knee-jerk reaction will be resentment ("Why do you guys demand so much of my time?") or self-criticism ("I'm so stupid. Why do I let people eat up all of my time?") or both. To prevent this sort of explosion, **set aside an hour each month to target one of your most pressing problems, and then make sure to invite to the discussion at least one other person whom this problem affects**. Why? Because you'll take yourself seriously only when you see that someone else is relying on you to be smart.

How to Win As a Leader

Advisor: Your strength is your confidence. You seem to us a supremely capable leader: intuitive, opinionated, assured. And so we find ourselves turning to you to solve our problems.

- We like it that you lead by example. No job is too small for you to tackle. No problem is unworthy of your attention. You show us all that a great team is built out of lots of small, smart, detailed decisions.

- Remind us that our clients want us to have anticipated their practical needs. We know our product or service better than our clients do. We know when it works best and what to watch out for. The power of your team lies in us knowing which client might want this information and then sharing it with them before they've even asked for it.

- Ensure we understand why we are changing something, and work hard to help us believe it is a good idea to change. Sometimes it feels as if you want change for the sake of change. You'll get the best out of us only if you've taken the time to show us that the "platform" is indeed burning.

- Resist the temptation to solve all our problems. We know you can do it, but if you always step in to help us, we'll never learn to solve them ourselves. Though it gives us confidence knowing you can, there are times we'd just like the freedom to find our own way.

Marcus Buckingham

- When the way is unclear, we rely on you to provide specificity—specificity of purpose, of steps to take, of what we will find when we get there. This is invaluable to us. Keep communicating the way. All the time.

- Of course, you will never need to fake your self-assurance, but now and then, temper it with a little self-deprecation. It makes us feel closer to you. It humanizes you.

How to Win As a Manager

Advisor: Your strength is your common sense. I come to you to play out real-world "what-ifs." You are my most practical resource.

- I trust your recommendations because in most matters you are an expert. I know that you've done your research or are speaking from experience. This gives me great confidence. Invite me to share my own ideas or insights. I need to know that my unique experience is also of value.

- Encourage me to take some industry-specific courses that can deepen my own expertise. Then talk to me about how what I have learned can help my coworkers or clients.

- I love how practical you are when it comes to rewarding me. When I win an award, you don't just give me something generic, such as a gift certificate. Instead you'll offer something useful to me, such as working my shift or buying me the new program I've been clamoring for. This tells me that you understand what my life is like.

- You are decisive. This keeps the wheels turning. I could benefit from slowing down at certain points to evaluate progress and ensure I'm still aiming in the right direction.

- I trust you with my problems. I feel safe bringing them to you. You provide excellent advice. Encourage me to bring solutions with my problems. Ask me, "What have you already considered?" or "What do you think you should do?"

- You are practical, pragmatic, and decisive. Which is great; things get done. But now and then leave me space for some "what if" thinking. Allow me to tap into my own creativity.

How to Win in Sales

Advisor: Your strength is your ability to explain precisely why your product or solution is unique. You draw such clear and vivid distinctions.

- Become an expert in your competitors' products or services. Help me, your potential client, see and understand the critical differences between your offering and that of others. You will excel at drawing these distinctions.

- Give me a logical process to help me consider my options as I work through a problem. I will always appreciate how carefully and rationally you review with me the details that matter.

- Come armed to all meetings with more than one approach to the challenge I'm facing. You are at your most persuasive when you are showing me how you weigh one choice against the other. I won't always agree with you, but watching you think things through will help me think things through.

- Over time I will come to lean on you for input during times of uncertainty. During these times, intentionally offer yourself as a resource within your area of greatest expertise. (However, take care not to guide decisions where you aren't qualified.)

- Demonstrate that you know my or my company's particular challenges inside and out. Even if I haven't engaged you yet, your presenting me unique solutions to problems that my current supplier is trying to help me solve may be just what it takes for me to switch. Show that you know me.

How to Win in Client Service

Advisor: Your strength is that your advice is specific and clear.

- You don't skate around an issue I, your client, may be having with your product or service. Instead you confront my problem head-on and, most importantly, give me something concrete to do about it. From my perspective, the more concrete you can be the better.

- You always seem to have anticipated my needs. You have researched my situation, pinpointed practical opportunities, seen the potential obstacles, and more often than not, plotted out my alternative courses of action. All of this "advance work" builds my confidence in you and your team.

- Limit my choices, as in "Do this or do that." This directness works for you—and for me. It keeps things simple and prevents me from second-guessing myself later.

- Be clear when you believe I've made a poor buying decision, and redirect me toward something that will serve my needs better. Make sure you give me at least three solid reasons for this advice.

- Get to know the details of the product or service inside and out. Share these details with me. I may not always understand exactly what you are saying, but the more obvious your expertise is, the more confident I will become.

- Be honest when you don't know the answer or cannot solve my problem right away. I love your confidence, but mine will quickly disappear if I sense that you're making things up.

- Speak my language. Learn the terms that I use to describe my world (client rather than customer, associates rather than salespeople) and ensure you always use this terminology when working with me. It shows me that you get that each client is unique and that you cater to that uniqueness.

CONNECTOR

The Definition

You begin by asking, *"Whom can I connect?"* You see the world as a web of relationships, and you are excited by the prospect of connecting people within your web. Not because they will like each other—though they might—but rather because of what they will create together. Your mantra is "One and one makes three" or thirty or three hundred. On your most optimistic days, you see almost no limit to what people with different strengths and perspectives can create together.

You are a naturally inquisitive person, always asking questions about each person's background, experience, and skills. You know instinctively that each person brings something unique and distinct to the table, something, no matter how small, that might prove to be the vital ingredient.

In your head, or in your contacts, you store a large network of people whom you've met, learned about, catalogued, and positioned somewhere within this network—each person with a link to at least one other person, and each with an open port for another link to be added. People are drawn to you because you are so obviously passionate about their particular expertise, and because you have so many practical ideas about how their expertise can be combined with others. You enliven and enlarge others' vision of who they are and what they can achieve. You are a connector, weaving people together into the fabric of something much larger and more significant than themselves.

You, at Your Most Powerful

- You think in terms of possibilities. "Wouldn't it be great if we linked up this person with that person?"

- You are a multiplier, always trying to put two things together to make something bigger and better than it is now.

- Your chief impact is through your sense of what could be, your excitement about the combination of people or of people plus technologies, projects, ideas.

- You create culture change, not because you talk "culture" but because you bring people together in order to get something done—you sense that there's no better way to get people to trust one another than to have them do work together.

- You bring new people on to a team quickly. Because you are able to "ramp up" people so fast, you make teams and organizations stronger, quicker.

- You are a catalyst. You speed up the reaction between two people or two groups or between a particular person and a particular challenge.

- You are a researcher of people. You are intrigued by people's unique qualities and talents, and so when you meet someone, you delve deep, asking one question after another. The more you understand about this person, the better you'll be able to position them so that they link up with others—either inside or outside the organization.

- You are also a researcher of facts, technologies, and products. Each new thing you learn is raw material. You can use it to make some new concoction of people, products, ideas.

- You are resourceful. When your back is against the wall, you are sure that you will know someone you can call. Your "toolbox" of people is big and always getting bigger.

- This resourcefulness gives you an aura of confidence—and of optimism. You have a strongly positive outlook about the world and about people in general. You just know that with enough thought you will be able to dredge your memory banks and find someone who can get it done.

- Others are drawn to you. They are drawn to you because they see that you are looking for their best qualities. They are drawn to you because you will connect them with people who can complement them. They are drawn to you because you find ways in which they can be useful.

- You are winning and persuasive. People tend to do what you ask of them because you excel at painting the picture of "what could be."

How to Describe Yourself (in Interviews, Performance Reviews)

- "I am fascinated by people's strengths and gifts."

- "I'm really good at figuring out who should work together and why they would work well together."

- "I'm a collector. I collect information about people and store it away so that I always know whom to call. For example . . ."

- "I love pulling people together from all parts of the organization for a special project. Here's how I did it in my last position . . ."

- "The most important thing to me is speed. I want to get myself up to speed on any new subject really quickly, and I want to find the right person to connect to this subject really quickly."

- "I get a kick out of 'wouldn't it be great if . . .' kind of thinking. I'm always cooking up new projects and plans."

- "I think I'm effective at persuading people to put aside their differences and join forces to get something done together."

How to Make an Immediate Impact

- You're lucky. You're a fast starter. Your natural instincts cause you to reach out and connect with your new colleagues. Your genuine interest in them will doubtless endear you to them. **So begin by letting these instincts run.**

- **Start building your own private "scouting report" on your new network.** For each person, capture what you've learned about his or her particular area of expertise or interest or experience, and your initial thoughts about where he or she adds the greatest value to the team.

- **Find an opportunity to surprise a colleague with how useful your network is.** Most people don't continually add people to their mental list of potential resources and so won't have many people whom they can call on to help them get something done or solve a problem. But you do. So as soon as you can find the right situation, pull out your "Rolodex" and offer just the right person or expert who can help solve a pressing problem.

- Once you feel you've had the chance to display your resourcefulness, it will be time to **flex your "possibility-thinking" muscles**. (Don't try this before you've established your credibility or others may reject your ideas as presumptuous.) What's powerful about you is that the possibilities you see in your head are not theoretical. Instead you think in terms of practical realities, as in "Let's put this person with that person and then focus them on this particular project." Your ideas might not necessarily

53

be accepted immediately, but persevere. Keep offering up these "what-if" scenarios. Soon your colleagues will come to rely on you as a source of practical ideas.

- Be sure to **target these "what-if" ideas toward solving existing problems** rather than creating something utterly new. People tend to be immediately grateful to problem solvers. And, in contrast, people are initially suspicious of innovators.

- **Always keep your social networking platforms up-to-date with fresh and vivid content**. You're inclined to do this anyway, but sometimes, as with all of us, the other demands in your life distract you. As the Connector amongst us, we will come to rely on you to maintain the web of our relationships. (If keeping three or four platforms up to date proves too much of a time drain, configure one platform so that it updates all the others.)

How to Take Your Performance to the Next Level

- **Stay attentive**. Wherever you go there's the chance to make a connection. Interesting people are everywhere, not just at work or at professional gatherings, but sitting next to you on the plane, at your child's birthday party, at the church planning meeting.

- You are inspired by extremely talented people, so try to **find at least two groups of experts in which you can play a leadership or organizing role**. It doesn't really matter what the group's expertise is. What's invigorating for you is hearing the discussions, listening to the different viewpoints of these "masters." Listen long enough and you will almost certainly come up with a new mission, a new possibility.

- **Discipline yourself to connect someone to something every day**. For example, send an e-mail a day beginning "I thought of you when I read this . . ." and then include a line or two about how this particular person might benefit or learn from what you sent them. We rely on you for practical possibility thinking, so be sure to draw a clear connection between what you sent and what the person might be able to do with it.

- To expand your network, **go beyond your usual haunts and gatherings**. Once or twice a year, sign up for an exciting group experience—a cycling trip, a charity walk, a river rafting expedition—and go alone. Given your nature, it's almost guaranteed that you'll encounter someone who'll spark an idea of a new connection you can make.

- People are always going to be attracted to you because of the possibilities you see in them and in what they can create with others. **Become better at describing these possibilities**—more vivid in your descriptions, more detailed in your explanations of why and how two people will complement each other so well—and you will grow to be extraordinarily effective at getting people to act on your ideas.

- When you are researching a subject, find the ultimate article, book, or paper; read the bibliography, identify the most frequently quoted sources, and then **reach out to these sources and get to know them**.

- Obviously everyone within your network does not have the same level of influence—some are higher leverage than others. **Identify the highest-leverage people in your web** and discipline yourself to have a meaningful conversation with them each month.

- Always act on the assumption that people—even very accomplished, famous people—want to connect with you. **If you've been impressed by a product, find out the inventor and call him or her. If you've enjoyed a book, reach out to the author**. Of course, they may not respond immediately, but with each e-mail or note from you, you are inching them toward the threshold when they will. And even if your "reach-outs" are never returned, rest assured that the person is reading them and appreciating them and that, if nothing else, your interest will encourage them to create more.

What to Watch Out For

- The difference between a name-dropper and a network builder is follow-up. What's powerful about you isn't who is in your network, **it's your ability to link up seemingly unconnected people within your network to make something happen**. People will get excited when you tell them you know someone who can help them; they will be disappointed when you don't make the call. Their disappointment will start to tarnish your reputation.

- When you connect people, do it well—this means **be detailed and specific**. When you introduce people to one another, paint a vivid picture of the strengths or experiences of each person, why you think each person complements the other, and what you think might be possible if they worked together. People are busy and it's hard to get their attention. Nothing succeeds in grabbing attention quite as well as detail.

- **Ask permission before you connect people**. Each of us is protective of our time. If you are careless or haphazard in linking up people, they may come to see you as a danger to their time, and wall themselves off from you and your ideas.

- **Don't become a "forwarder."** Never send out a mass e-mail in the hopes that someone, somewhere within your network, will benefit from it. This is the laziest form of network building. It reveals that you see us as an undifferentiated mass of people. This will annoy us.

- **Try not to be disappointed if people don't call you back**. Some people need a lot of nudging before they will respond to your invitations. So long as each "reach-out" is done with detail—"Here's exactly what I was thinking . . ."—each nudge will come across as respectful and will move them just a little bit closer to responding.

- When you are identifying high-leverage people within your network, remember that sometimes the most important person in an organization—be it a company, a community group, or a "movement"—is the number two. The number one might be the original idea guy, the visionary, the rallying point. But **the second person to join the "movement" is actually the person whose connections run deeper into the organization**. This is the person you need to know if you want to make things happen.

How to Win As a Leader

Connector: Your strength is your ability to see the best in us. We sense that if we stick with you, you will make us a vital part of something significant. And so we are drawn to you.

- Tell us how important it is to you for our company to be a "friend in the community." We all want to know that we are a part of something bigger than ourselves—a community of people and businesses who rely on one another. You help us see these connections.

- Show us the practical things we can do to connect with our community. Challenge us to think of new ways to reach out to our neighbors. Join local charities. Shred our newspapers and ask us to give them to the SPCA. Tell us to take our old towels to the local firehouse. Can we give our old equipment to Habitat for Humanity? Can we sponsor or participate in a local sporting event for charity?

- You are at your best in a crisis. We know we'll never be left in a lurch because you know someone, who knows someone, who knows someone who can get the job done. At staff meetings tell us the stories of how we handled it "when the storm blew out the electricity for twelve hours." These stories will inspire us and give us the confidence that we can cope with any situation or emergency.

- You're always thinking about the people, ideas, and technologies you could combine to create something new. We love this because it gives us security. We know there are fresh experiences and projects waiting in the wings. Strengthen our security by telling us regularly about the connections you've made.

- In your desire to find the perfect mix of people to get the job done, you break down barriers between people and departments. This will scare some people. Know this, and then learn how to show them what can be gained.

- Keep your connections fresh and new. Include novel and unexpected minds in some of your mixes. We like to know we might be next.

- You're a masterful delegator. Just make sure we witness you rolling up your sleeves too. We need to know that you're as willing and able to commit yourself to the job as we are.

How to Win As a Manager

Connector: Your strength is building surprisingly talented teams. I know I can count on you to do your due diligence when cherry-picking new teammates.

- Your natural reaction is to look outside the company to the people we are trying to serve—the client. Remind me of this mission. This seems obvious, but sometimes the details of my own position distract me.

- At staff meetings or during one-on-ones, describe for me in detail what the client's life is like. Tell me about their concerns, their agendas, their budgets. I may have never sat on their side of the table before. You can help me see the world through their eyes.

- I like seeing you out with our clients virtually all the time. The way you engage directly with their lives, the way you sort out their problems, the way you speak their "language," all of this reinforces the ultimate purpose of my job.

- You take the time to discover the unique talents required for a vacant spot—you're in no hurry to "just fill it." Thank you for never settling, but instead, for always looking for the right and best person. We need you to remind us that this is how great teams are built—one good person at a time.

- You have such a wide network of people, you always know someone who's been successful at what I'm currently tackling. Whenever I am stuck on something, use your network to give me ideas for how to get unstuck.

- You trust me with key projects. You have faith in my ability to solve problems. I love this freedom. I also need to know that you are there as support. Now and then, check in on my progress.

- Be careful in your comparisons. You can tend to evaluate me against my teammates or other people you've worked with. I need to know that you see me for my own particular abilities.

How to Win in Sales

Connector: Your strength is your active network of relationships. Your need to reach out and stay current with your network will help those you have selected feel valued and appreciated.

- As your potential client I like it when you come around and visit me. You've always got something going on, some news to share about what your company is doing or what is going on in our industry. Your network offers me access to valuable resources I would not be able to find on my own.

- You seem to me to have a wide network. I'd love to meet some of the other people in your network. Can you put on a lunch or a dinner, some event where we can all get to know one another? Organize meetings, retreats, off-sites, learning seminars, symposia. We want to belong. We want to feel part of a smart group who can learn from one another. You can be our host and our bond, tying us together and to you.

- Always take the time to ensure that the people you introduce me to can really help me. As this happens more and more, I will see you as more and more credible.

- Your referrals will always be one of your powerful sales weapons. Sort through your network and organize it into different layers or levels of "referral." Some you will use for first-time buyers. Others you will call upon only when you want to cast a vision of a full-blooded, multiyear partnership.

- Personalize all your interactions with me. If you're pushing out a mass mail-out campaign, make sure to cross out the "Dear Ms. So-and-so" and handwrite my first name in. Scribble a few lines in the margin about how you're looking forward to seeing me on the twenty-first. Show me that I'm not just one *of* a million, I'm one *in* a million.

How to Win in Client Service

Connector: Your strength is your resourcefulness. You always have some person or some idea that can help solve my situation.

- You leave no stone unturned. I can tell you're working as hard as possible to find solutions for me, your client. Tell me the steps you're taking. I need to follow your line of thinking.

- You really listen to my needs. You are loyal to your brand, but what I like about you is that you don't hesitate to introduce an alternate brand or product if you think it will serve my needs better. I appreciate this because it reassures me that you care more about my satisfaction than filling a quota.

- I like it that you deal with my problems head-on. I sense that you are a resourceful person who will be able to nip my problem in the bud, or who will know the person to call to help me solve it.

- You are effective at offering additional services that you know will truly boost my experience. Be very clear on the benefits and potential drawbacks of these add-ons. The better you get at this, the more I will feel that it is a legitimate enhancement rather than an up-sell.

- You think of me as a person first, a client second. You never forget my name and always make a point of recalling a fact from a previous conversation. This connection reassures me that you have my best interests in mind, because you have paid attention to me. Develop a system—a place to capture names, details, specifics about me and other customers—to hone this talent.

- Make me feel like an insider. When possible, invite me behind the curtain and let me see some of your inner workings. I may not always take you up on the offer but that you trust me this much does not go unnoticed. It will be reciprocated in my repeat business.

CREATOR

The Definition

You begin by asking, *"What do I understand?"* You aren't immune to the feelings and perspectives of others, but your starting point is your own insight, your own understanding. You see the world as a series of collisions between competing parts, pieces, and agendas; and you are compelled to figure it all out. For you there's nothing quite as thrilling as finding a pattern beneath life's complexities, a core concept that can explain why things play out the way they do, or better yet, predict how things are *going* to play out.

You are a thoughtful person, someone who needs time alone to mull and muse—without this alone time, events pile up on you haphazardly, and your confusion starts to overwhelm you. So you look forward to time by yourself—early in the morning, late at night, long walks—and you use this time to get clear. You are a creative person. What form this creativity takes will depend on your other traits and talents, but whether you write, paint, sing, complete projects, or make presentations, you are drawn toward making things. Each thing you make is a tangible sign that you have made some sense of the world, that you have organized the chaos in some useful way. You look at what you've made, you take pleasure in what you now understand, and then you move on to the next creation.

You, at Your Most Powerful

- Your power comes from making sense of things.

- When you look at the world, you can't help but see beneath the surface to the patterns underneath. You are intrigued by patterns. Patterns help you explain (to yourself, as much as to anyone else) what is going on.

- This is why you like concepts. Concepts are the best explanation for most events. Your world is full of concepts that you've derived from your observations of the world.

- You take great pride in your ideas. You are protective of them. They are the best expression of you.

- Your world is thrown off when you don't understand what is going on. When presented with an unfamiliar situation you need time—time to process, to observe, to ask your questions, to think things through. "Don't ask me to make snap judgments," you protest. "Let me gather my thoughts."

- You don't like surprises. You don't like making things up as you go along. When you make things—and you do like to make things—you do it only after you've had time to percolate and process.

- You certainly are creative, but you don't conjure things out of thin air. You break things down into their component elements and this enables you to reconfigure them in new and different ways. Thus you are always watching and observing so that you can identify these elements.

- You aren't bothered by ambiguity, by gaps in the "data." Instead you instinctively create theories out of the facts you do have at your disposal, and then you allow your theory to fill in the gaps in the facts. As such, your thinking is inferential rather than deductive.

- You are prone to flashes of insight into a better way of doing things or presenting things. Reflecting back, it's hard for you to explain quite where these flashes came from, but once you've seen them, you cannot get them out of your mind. The need to make them real propels you forward. (Once you've seen this flash, you will need a partner to help you work backward to the step-by-step sequence required to make the "flash" real.)

- You are relentless. Though at the outset you will not be rushed, as you think on it and think on it, the patterns emerge, these patterns create theories, the theories spark new insights, and all of a sudden you are being borne along by these pictures in your mind. You take a while to get going, but once you are off and running, you are hard to stop.

How to Describe Yourself (in Interviews, Performance Reviews)

- "I've been told I'm a very creative person, always looking for better ways of doing things."

- "I love theories, concepts. People often come to me when they want someone to explain why things are playing out the way they are."

- "I ask 'why?' a lot. I guess it can get annoying sometimes, but I can't help it. I'm the kind of person who hates assumptions. I need to get to the bottom of why things are the way they are."

- "I'm at my best when I'm analyzing what happened and why it happened."

- "I read a lot—both fiction and nonfiction. Why? Because I like it. And because it keeps my mind full of ideas."

- "Someone once told me that creativity comes only to the prepared mind, so I read, study, and ask questions so my mind is prepared."

- "I don't like rushing into things. I'm not a ready, fire, aim person. I'm more a study, ready, aim, fire, study again person."

How to Make an Immediate Impact

- It is going to take you a little time to make your full impact felt. Before you feel confident taking action, you need to understand the forces at play and how these forces combine to create patterns. This kind of pattern recognition takes time. You need this time. **Be patient**.

- You can't force pattern recognition but you can accelerate it. So, no matter what your other job responsibilities, **discipline yourself to uncover the patterns**. Which data will you look to, to reveal what's really going on? Which outcomes keep repeating? If you see range in performance between one person and another or between one team and another, can you spot the prime mover that is causing this range? Investigate these tell-tale signs to reveal the patterns.

- When you feel ready, pick an area where you have confidence that you've decoded the patterns that matter, and then **use your understanding of these patterns to present to your colleagues a better way of doing things**. What you're doing here is trying to make your understanding useful as quickly as possible. There's pressure in this, of course—will you be able to refine your thinking so that it is clear and actionable?—but you're the kind of person who will feel this as positive pressure, even fun pressure. Your ideas won't necessarily be accepted right away, but your reputation for thoughtfulness will have begun.

- If your initial idea is rejected, find another place or situation where your first key concept can also be applied.

What's powerful about an understanding is that it is transferable from situation to situation.

- As any Creator must, it is your responsibility to **figure out what your raw material is**. A Creator has to work with something and get good at working with something. So what is your "something"? Is it words or data or deals or is it something tangible—food, color, or metals?

- And whatever it is, **do you know whether, within your chosen "something," you are a novelty-loving Creator or a depth-loving Creator**? Neither is better, but you will undoubtedly find yourself pulled more toward one than the other. If novelty, then you will want to cultivate the reputation for learning agility—"Throw me in and I'll spot the patterns quickly." If depth, then take it upon yourself to show off your expertise in your subject—learn the jargon; retrieve the latest writings, research, works; and resist the intriguing temptations of other subjects, other "somethings."

- **Always produce**. Of course you feel driven to produce, to create something, but your production, your output, is also the raw material for future creations. Your output will show you (and others) what sense you've made, the patterns you've discovered and rearranged, and when you (and others) see this output, it will jolt your thinking and give you impetus for new patterns, new arrangements. A Creator must always externalize—"put out there"—the patterns he or she sees.

- **In the same vein, get to know your audience**. Who are you producing for, and have you set up your world so that you are constantly hearing their unadulterated response to your output? Response doesn't necessarily mean praise—though it might. It means simply their reaction. Their reaction will be grist for your creative mill. "Which bit exactly are they reacting to?" you will ask yourself. You won't always agree with or even credit their reaction, but it will nonetheless give you meaty raw material to work with.

- **Read**. Stay current on new trends, research, or practices within your chosen "something." You've got to know who the latest Creators are and what new sense they are making of the world.

How to Take Your Performance to the Next Level

- **Take time to muse**. You need time alone to let your mind live with the things you've seen and what you've experienced, so it can settle into some sort of shape. This thinking time is vital to your well-being—without it, you feel confused and on edge. It is also vital to your performance—it is the ground from which will spring new insights and discoveries. Take it very seriously. You need it. Others don't, and they won't quite understand why you do. So build it into your schedule and stick to it religiously. It doesn't have to be so frequent that it interferes with your daily work. It just has to be predictable—you are comforted knowing that thinking time is coming.

- As a Creator you will have to **figure out how to "own" your creations**. At one extreme, this might mean working only in fields where you are allowed to own the intellectual property you create, such as journalism or entertainment. Or you might work for a large organization only if they allow you to write papers under your name or file for patents under your name. If neither of these is a possibility for you, still you will need to figure out a way to "sign" your work.

- **Create a forum for safe experimentation**, a place where you can share new, as yet fragile, patterns of understanding. It could be a cross-industry group of like-minded thinkers. It could be an informal Skunk Works within your own organization. Wherever it is, it should be comprised of people who question you and challenge you with no agenda other than helping you to strengthen (or break) the sense you've made. This group will become your testing ground.

- **Stick your neck out**. What is your highest-leverage "creation," the one with the greatest exposure and risk, yet the greatest potential upside? In other words, what is your home run?

- **Seek out the "enemy camp."** Deliberately forge a relationship with people who see things very differently from you. They may discredit the sense you make. They may even disparage your work. And you may still disagree with them. But by exposing yourself to them, you will prevent yourself from becoming complacent.

- In this enemy camp, **look for evidence that contradicts what you've come to believe**. Faced with this, you will either become more articulate in explaining your point of view or you will discredit the contradictory evidence or you will expand your view to incorporate this evidence. Each of these is, in its own way, a positive outcome.

What to Watch Out For

- While you are studying your world and figuring out the patterns, you still have to be doing. The world will not wait for you to figure it all out. Nor will your colleagues. Nor will your customers. So, **whatever patterns you're looking for, you're going to have to figure them out in the world, as you're doing**.

- Others can become discouraged or disillusioned by ideas that don't quite work. It will be up to you to **show them that the experiment itself will have value, regardless of the outcome**. Before you present your idea, discipline yourself to describe in detail what could be learned even from the worst-case scenario outcome.

- **Don't ever gain the reputation for being the chief "defender of the idea."** The defender of the idea is the person from whom one always gets the same answer, the person whose creative back is up against the wall, the person who has closed his or her mind to new information. You do not want to be this person. You want to be seen as the person who, despite your strongly held views and insights, is always open to new data, new evidence, new patterns of understanding.

- Having said this, remember **"open," in this instance, means "inquisitive."** It does not mean "immediately accepting of." The balance you have to strike is between staunchly opinionated at one extreme and, at the other, wishy-washy theorizing. We tend to avoid the former, and we're suspicious of the latter. The perfect middle ground is to be seen as inquisitive.

How to Win As a Leader

Creator: Your strength is your ability to think things through. As our leader, we see your mind working and it gives us confidence. We know you will make a new sense of things.

- You have incredible ideas. Share your vision with us. What are you creating next? What's so exciting about it? Why should we go along?

- You excel at keeping it simple. No need for complex graphs or excessive business terminology. When you set a goal, make it clear to all of us why it's important and what part we play in achieving it. Then, keep that goal in front of us and link everything back to it. Show us how it all ties together.

- Demonstrate your passion for the client's experience. Show us how simple and easy it can be to make a client feel special. We will share these stories with our colleagues. It makes us proud to align with a leader who cuts through the complexity and reveals how simple it can be to do the right thing.

- Trust us. At times your need to understand everything that's going on or to control the process slows us down. We don't mind reporting on progress, but it can distract us from getting the job done. You recruited really good people; let us prove it to you.

- We feel secure with your deliberate nature. We know you've asked a million "why"s before presenting a solution or idea to us. We would love to be privy to your process or, better yet, at times included. We feel more connected to work that we had a say in creating.

- Teach and model that when it's true, the best answer is "I don't know, but I'll find out." We appreciate your humility, that you don't have unreasonable expectations of yourself or any of us. This vulnerability makes it easier for us to connect to you. Also, when you defer to your experts, it creates opportunities for other team members to shine.

- Sometimes you can insulate yourself. We know this is because your mind needs solitude to be productive. Just make sure that you do come up for air often enough for us to connect to you. The sense you create is exciting to us. We need to see you.

How to Win As a Manager

Creator: Your strength is the time you give me. To listen. To consider. To understand before reaching your conclusions.

- When issues arise, take the time to consider all perspectives and investigate what's been done to address the problem to date. I'll appreciate that when something goes wrong, you don't jump right into fixing but acknowledge and salvage my efforts.

- Seek out spontaneous opportunities to explain to us how our actions and efforts are making a difference for our clients. Keep tying what we do back to the "why" of our work. We, your employees, will not go down the street to another company for dollars if we know that what we do here really matters.

- Be crystal clear and consistent with your expectations. Check that we understand by asking us to repeat back what we've heard. With this clarity in place, when we're off track we can self-correct before a curative conversation ever needs to occur. No performance correction should ever come as a surprise.

- You create momentum. It's incredible to be along for the ride once one of your ideas takes off. Keep communicating what you're seeing and I'll keep supporting our progress.

- I want to learn from you. Your process of dismantling and solving problems, of seeing patterns in the most complex data, fascinates me. Let me peek behind the curtain: share your process.

- Give credit where credit is due. Even though the initial idea was often yours, it's really important that I hear you acknowledge my contribution and the contributions of my teammates.

How to Win in Sales

Creator: Your strength is your sophistication. You will win sales through your deliberate timing. You know how to listen and fully understand before jumping in with your point of view.

- I, your potential client, love your poise and style. Because you are thoughtful and open-minded, I feel free to discuss my situation with you quite openly. Start these discussions with me and always allow me to say my piece. I will reach my own conclusions. You will be my guide.

- You crave time out to think. Honor this need and set time in your schedule to muse about the day. From these musings will come ideas and alternatives that neither your competitors nor I will have considered.

- At some point, I will need you to make a strong recommendation. Your need to consider all contingencies and possibilities may at times hold you back from pursuing a path with conviction. Push through the what-ifs and the what-abouts. You've thought it through, now go all out to turn your vision into reality.

- Choose opportunities for business development that require more than superficial understanding. You will thrive most where my situation and the sale within it are complex. Here you can drill down, carefully pick apart my situation, and pinpoint precisely why I am struggling and how you can best help me.

- While I appreciate your helping me with solutions for current needs, what's so valuable is the way you push me to also consider future needs. Keep informing me how the steps I'm taking with you today are setting me up to be ready for what's coming down the pike.

How to Win in Client Service

Creator: Your strength is that you take the time to discover the root cause of my need. You don't just provide me with the pat answer.

- You are skilled at asking relevant questions. Hone this, as it shows me that you're truly curious and interested in unpacking my problem. I won't get the sense that you're following some set of rules. Instead you'll make me feel that my situation is exceptional.

- You bring a thoughtfulness to your service. I don't mean you're caring—though you may be. I mean that I can see your mental wheels turning. When you're ready, let me in on your thinking. Tell me what conclusion you've arrived at.

- I appreciate your calmness. No matter how upset I might be, you manage to keep your cool. On the other hand, a sense of urgency at times would be welcome. Although I'm sure you're working on it, check in with me with status updates to reassure me that you're still "on my case."

- Trust your instincts. Just because the solution you've considered isn't in "the book" doesn't mean it isn't right. As your customer I will always appreciate signs that you are pushing the boundaries in order to solve my problem.

- Ask "what's working?" as often as you ask "what's broken?" If you get too caught up in fixing problems, I miss out on your ability to see growth opportunities. Keep me out of the minutiae and focused on the big possibilities.

EQUALIZER

The Definition

You begin by asking, *"What is the right thing to do?"* You are sensitive to how everything in the world is interdependent, how movement in one part of the world causes everything else to move as well. Alive to this interconnectedness, you feel compelled to keep everything aligned. This need for alignment might be organizational—you sense when your world is disorganized and you get a kick out of restoring everything back to its rightful place. Or it might be ethical—you are acutely aware of who is responsible for what, and you are quick to take action if someone doesn't live up to her responsibilities. You have no problem calling her out if she hasn't followed through, and you are just as willing to call yourself out when you drop the ball.

You see the commitments we make to one another as threads that connect us and allow us to share in each other's success. It pains you when you see these threads break, and so you are their passionate protector. At your best, you are our conscience, helping us realize how much we owe one another and how much we rely on one another. You hold us together.

You, at Your Most Powerful

- You are a levelheaded person. The world is best for you when it is in balance.

- Yours is a moral world made up of mutual obligations. You are driven to keep the balance in this moral world. You are unnerved when your world tips too far in any one direction.

- What tips your world out of balance?

  ○ When people don't tell the truth. You hate lying, or even half-truths. Politics and finessing are anathema to you. You feel strengthened by the truth and you tell the truth. Sometimes quite bluntly.

  ○ When there is ambiguity and uncertainty. You try to redress the balance by finding out more facts. Facts are solid.

  ○ When people do not follow through on their commitments. This bugs the heck out you. You will push them, or yourself, to do whatever it takes to ensure that the commitment is met. If it isn't, then the only way to pull the world back into balance is to make amends in some way.

  ○ When someone is wronged. Yours is a moral world, and so it offends you when someone's wrong is not righted. You are a passionate defender of people's rights, including your own.

○ Where you see huge disparities of reward and/or praise. You have a strong sense of the innate worth of each person, and it offends you when someone is raised up significantly higher than another. No matter how talented this person may be, it just doesn't seem right to you.

- You are a categorical person. Black and white. True or false. *Don't give me pretty pictures and grand claims*, you think to yourself. *Just tell me if you did it or you didn't.*

- You are predictable and consistent. At least you strive to be. This is why people come to trust you.

- People come to you when they want clarity and opinion. You weigh things in your mind and get a strong sense of what the *right* thing to do is in almost any situation.

- You think in terms of *who has the "right" to do this?* Rights and responsibilities are your guides. It offends you when you think that someone has overstepped their bounds and done something they have no right to do. You will fight for redress.

How to Describe Yourself (in Interviews, Performance Reviews)

- "I am a highly responsible person."

- "People always know where they stand with me, even if sometimes they don't like where they stand."

- "I am the kind of person who takes a stand for causes I deeply believe to be right, even if it puts me in the minority. For example, there was this time when . . ."

- "I'm at my best when I'm persuading people to see what is right and do what is right—even if they are tempted to do something else."

- "I hate unfinished work. It just eats at me. I can't stop thinking about it."

- "I'm totally transparent. What you see with me is what you get. I am not good at all with hidden agendas—whether my own, or other peoples'."

- "Sometimes I can be a little blunt with people, but I hope they come to see me as someone whom they can always trust to speak truthfully."

How to Make an Immediate Impact

- People like certainty. **Follow-through is the surest way to give them this certainty**. No matter how tempting it might be to look around the corner to the next opportunity, begin by being conservative about what you are prepared to commit to and then make sure you do what you say you are going to do—on time, on budget, no surprises. This will establish your reputation.

- **Claim your love of bringing order to things**. So many people shy away from disorder that it will be a relief for your colleagues to learn that someone on the team likes confronting disorder.

- **Speak your values**. This doesn't mean to tell everyone how honest you are—counterintuitively, the more you profess your honesty, the less people believe it to be true. It means be explicit about what you believe and what you value. Of course, your behavior is going to prove it out, but your beliefs are so much a part of who you are that talking about them will sound authentic.

- You are a truth teller. One of the first ways you'll make an impact is by **calling out what you see as inappropriate, ineffective, or even unethical behavior**. The good news is that soon people will come to realize that you don't merely parrot the party line, and over time they will trust what they hear from you. The downside, of course, is that some people will not like what you have to say, and some will feel judged by you. Especially at the start, find a way to speak your truth without offending the person on the receiving end. Call out the behavior you disagree with, rather than the person, for example, "It's hard to have this meeting if you keep showing up late" as opposed to "You don't care about this team, do you?"

- You have an instinctive sense of fairness, even on those occasions when your sense of fairness leads you to conclude that you don't deserve something you've been given. **This sort of objectivity, even when it leads to your disadvantage, is rare**. There will be opportunities to showcase it. Seek them out.

- **Help your colleagues find the right method for getting complex tasks done**. Some people get overwhelmed and can't think their way forward. You can show them how to break the tasks down and move ahead, step-by-step. Your methodical approach to work creates calm and reassurance in others.

- **Set up the right circumstances where people around you can be accountable**. This means that before the project starts or at the beginning of every week, be the one who pushes for clear goals and expectations for each team member.

- **Define your area of responsibility clearly**. You always function best when the boundaries of your position and others' positions are crystal clear. If necessary, write down these boundaries and make them explicit for you and your colleagues. You'll like this certainty and, whether they realize it or not, those around you will benefit from it.

How to Take Your Performance to the Next Level

- **Seek out situations where you can stand up for the rights of others**. You are in your zone when you do this. No matter what your talents may be in other aspects of your work, when it comes to explaining what people truly deserve, you will instinctively find the words and the arguments to make their case persuasively.

- **Establish your precedents**. When has this situation happened before? What were the outcomes? Who were the aggrieved parties? People will always look to you for a fair hearing, and your rationales will be better and clearer if you can point to previous experiences and situations.

- **Be thorough**. As your career progresses people will place more and more weight on your judgments. Always have at your disposal all the facts and, if possible, the data behind these facts. You need, and they need, to have confidence in your judgments. Lacking the facts and the data, you run the risk of being seen as merely judgmental.

- **Seek out situations where people need objective mediation**. Quite soon people will realize that you are a person who uses objective judgments—rather than your own personal goals or preferences—to determine right from wrong. The trusted advisor, the objective leader, the balanced analyst, these are all rare and valued roles that you are very well equipped to play.

- **Develop your skills as a mediator**. You have natural talent in this area, but to become a master at it will take time, practice, and, more than likely, education. There are professional mediation qualifications you can acquire, skills that will help you know how to move others off the rock of their opinion and find a place of common ground. Armed with these skills you will find yourself better able to navigate through even the most dug-in positions.

What to Watch Out For

- **When you say you want people to be treated fairly, what exactly do you mean**? We, your colleagues, need to know. Do you mean that everyone should be treated exactly the same? Or do you mean that each person should be treated as they deserve to be treated, bearing in mind who they are and what they have accomplished for the organization? Clearly, these are very different definitions of fairness. Which is yours?

- **Be sure to apply your methodical approach to your own physical space**. You tend to think best when you have some order around you. Take this seriously. You will have better ideas and be more productive and resilient when you sense that your world—and the stuff in your world—is in its rightful place.

- **Keep your focus on performance**. Occasionally your sense of fairness might lead you to overemphasize *how* someone gets work done and to ignore *what* he or she gets done.

- **Make a list of the rules of fairness by which you can live**. These rules might be based upon certain values that you have or upon certain policies that you consider non-negotiables within your organization. Counter-intuitively, the clearer you are about these rules, the more comfortable you will be with granting exceptions within these boundaries. If these rules or values are not explicit, people are left having to infer the grid you are using to make your judgments. This can make you appear arbitrary in your judgments—even if you aren't.

How to Win As a Leader

Equalizer: Your strength is the structure you bring us. We need a foundation, a grid, a framework within which to create. We turn to you for guidance.

- We trust you to do the right thing. You are so transparent about this value that it gives us confidence that we're aligned behind an ethical and forthright individual. You do what you say you are going to do when you say you are going to do it. We love this about you. Protect this reputation above all else.

- Life moves so quickly that we can get lost. We rely on you to tell us what you are certain of, what we can rely on. Your discipline is the catalyst for our creativity, our experiments in how to go above and beyond what the client or our colleagues expect.

- Pay attention to the team's energy. If you can't get a sense for it, find a trusted partner to help you gauge it. Sometimes you miss important clues about how we feel because you're so focused on direction or process. Create a team-member panel to allow direct interaction with a group of frontliners. This is a great opportunity for us to share what it really feels like here. Be sure to keep it casual and we'll open right up.

- Show us your personality. We sometimes feel we don't really know you. Take the time to tell personal stories and we'll feel more connected. You don't have to be the entertainer at the front of the room, just look for opportunities to make personal connections as you walk the office or share our successes.

- Ensure we're prepared. Clearly articulate the what, how, and why of quality and the steps we need to take to maximize it. Create opportunities for us to practice activities that might be expected of us. That way, when it comes time to measure the quality of our work, we won't fear this event; we will look forward to it.

- Acknowledge when it is time to give up on an idea, project, or person. Your commitment to finishing what you started can sometimes blind you to negative realities.

How to Win As a Manager

Equalizer: Your strength is the certainty you give me. I always know what to expect from you, and so my relationship with you is predictable and therefore secure.

- You work hard. I see how committed you are to getting things done, and this encourages me to contribute my best to help achieve our mutual goals.

- I can count on you. If you make a decision or a promise to me, I know that you'll see it through. Keep the same integrity around your meetings and one-on-ones. The more I see that these are meaningful to you and not simply an activity that you tolerate, the more present and accountable I will be.

- Revisit SMART (Specific Measurable Actionable Relevant Timebound) plans every three months without fail. The clarity and certainty this provides me as your employee keeps me focused and engaged. It also speaks to your dedication to my development and success at the company, and so increases my loyalty.

- Support our training and lead by example by keeping yourself up-to-date as well. Take over for us now and then to keep abreast of system changes and challenges. Also, if you're able to use a system more efficiently than we are, that's probably a good opportunity for you to give us additional support and training.

- You are thorough and organized. I'm confident that what you assign is what needs to be done. This frees me to focus without concern that my efforts will end up on the cutting room floor.

- You treat people fairly. You consider how decisions will impact workloads. You evaluate how to distribute bonuses equitably. You ensure that acknowledgments are universal. You do your best to keep things equal. Sometimes, though, note when I've gone above and beyond and look for a special way to recognize me.

How to Win in Sales

Equalizer: Your strength is your responsibility. Keep doing exactly what you say you are going to do, and soon you will have established the kind of trusting relationships that your competitors will find hard to break.

- In all aspects of work, your standards of equity and justice guide the way you do business. Your principled approach builds credibility as we, your clients, come to rely on your integrity.

- You feel intense accountability to make good on a promise or commitment you have made. Your obligation to fulfill commitments pushes you to find a way to follow through and deliver. Your resourcefulness sets you apart.

- Take the lead in structuring the proposal. You attend to the details that matter. I will notice this careful planning and will want to return to it when I am thinking about a future purchase.

- Your judgments are fair and appropriate. Your levelheaded style will serve you well as you manage through the challenges of an account relationship. I will always know I will get a fair hearing from you.

- Be careful about putting down your competitors when you believe they're behaving unethically. I don't need to be caught up in the drama. Just tell me what makes your solution different and why I need it.

How to Win in Client Service

Equalizer: Your strength is your sense of fairness. I can rely on you to do what is right.

- I trust you. You tell me the good news. You tell me the bad news. You don't put a positive spin on a negative reality. You just tell it like it is. At times I'd appreciate a little more empathy, but I'll always take the truth over sugarcoating.

- You do what you say you are going to do when you say you are going to do it. I value this immensely. I may not always get the answer that I'm hoping for, but at least I'm not wasting my time waiting.

- Set a standard for follow-up and communicate that to me. When I provide feedback about my experience at your company, whether positive or negative, tell me when I can expect to hear back from someone. Keep the time frame as short as possible. This shows me you respect me and genuinely care about my experience.

- You follow the rules. At times I wish you would bend them to suit me, but I do appreciate the assurance that the next customer is not going to get a better deal or a different answer than I am. This level playing field calms me and gives me confidence.

- On the other hand, not every situation deserves the same response, so be inquisitive. Take the time to ask your questions in order to discover what might be different about my particular situation.

- Acknowledge a legitimate gripe. I can sense that you care I'm treated fairly, so always admit when your product or service has missed the mark. You'll keep my business.

INFLUENCER

The Definition

You begin by asking, *"How can I move you to act?"* In virtually every situation, your eye goes to the outcome. Whether you are in a long meeting at work, helping a colleague get his work done, or talking a friend off a ledge, you measure your success by your ability to persuade the other person to do something he didn't necessarily intend to do. You may do this by the force of your arguments, your charm, your ability to outwit him, or perhaps by some combination of all of these. But regardless of your method, what really matters to you is moving the other person to action.

Why? Partly because you see where things will lead if the other person doesn't act, and partly because you are instinctively aware of momentum and become frustrated when you bump into someone who slows your momentum down—but mostly because you just can't help it. It's simply fun for you to influence people's behavior through the power of your personality. It's challenging and mysterious and thrilling and in the end, of course, it makes good things happen.

You, at Your Most Powerful

- In any situation you set your sights on action. "What can we *do*?" This is your question.

- You are, in general, impatient; but you are especially impatient when you know that a decision should be made. You see what will happen if we don't act. You see around the corner, and so it burns you to think about what inaction will cause.

- Others feel you are persuasive. You engage with them directly and you convince them. All of your relationships have this quality—you, moving others to act.

- You are driven by the feeling of progress and are acutely sensitive to momentum. You sense when it's building, when it's peaking, and when it's gone.

- You listen well, but you listen for a reason: either so that the person can talk herself into a place where she is psychologically ready to act, or so that you hear which triggers to pull in order to propel the person to make a decision. Listening, for you, is a precursor to action.

- You can be a charmer and are good at winning people over so that they like you. You do this because you know that people are willing to do more for those they like. Being liked is a powerful (though not the only) precondition for getting the other person to make a decision.

- You can be very direct. You feel strongly that problems are solved only when they are confronted head-on. You are not interested in dancing around a subject. Instead you use conflict as your preferred method of resolution.

- When you meet resistance you become energized. You know you get better when people give you reasons why they can't act. Each reason is something for you to engage with, something you can grab on to and use to get them to see why making a decision is so necessary.

- People sense your desire to move forward, and it comes across as self-assurance—even confidence. Occasionally as arrogance. Sometimes you might even put others off by challenging them more than you should—meaning "more than they would like to be challenged."

- People realize that you have an agenda. And people like you most, indeed trust you most, when your agenda is clear.

How to Describe Yourself (in Interviews, Performance Reviews)

- "I've found that I'm more decisive than most people—and more impatient. I like to move fast."

- "I'm at my best when I'm challenged to persuade someone to do something they didn't necessarily intend to do."

- "I initiate a lot. I'm always telling my colleagues what they should do. I suppose sometimes I might push too much, but we always get a lot done."

- "I hate playing politics. I'm a very up-front person and don't function well in a world with a lot of backroom action."

- "I get a thrill from the 'ask.' What's the worst they can say? 'No.' Well, so what? The sun's going to rise again tomorrow."

- "People seem to want to do more for me and with me than they do for other people. I enjoy getting people on my side."

- "I don't like talking around a subject. I like getting to the point. I think that's one of my strengths: focusing people on what the *outcome* is."

How to Make an Immediate Impact

- You are instinctively impatient. To ensure this doesn't rub your new colleagues the wrong way, **pick a roadblock that everyone agrees on and volunteer to be the one to tackle it**. For example, if there is something your team wants, but someone—a manager, a client, a colleague— has always stood in the way of getting it, then volunteer to make the call and make the 'ask.' Who knows, perhaps you'll prove persuasive. Perhaps you won't. Either way you'll have shown your nerve.

- Initially, because you are so action focused, people will wonder what your agenda is. So, to stop their wondering, be explicit with your teammates about it. **Tell them your agenda**. It doesn't really matter what your agenda is—it could be making the sale, stirring things up, or getting your way. What matters is that you are transparent about it. People don't mind persuasiveness. What they don't like is uncertainty. And without a clear agenda, sometimes your persuasive push can feel like manipulation.

- **Look for ways to measure your results**. You will be energized by the "proof" of whether you're ahead or behind. You are always at your best when you know exactly where you stand.

- Whenever you succeed in making something happen, **be deliberate in thanking people for their help**. If you don't do this, they may come to feel as though they are merely instruments in your plan of action. So tell them how much you valued their contribution. Spread this goodwill. Sometime soon it will come back to you and with their cooperation smoothing the way, you will be able to make more decisions.

- Listen. Look engaged. Ask short, open-ended questions and then keep quiet. Show interest in what the other person is saying. Be seen to be taking notes. All of this will let the other person feel heard and allow you to establish some kind of relationship before you dive into your agenda. This relationship will then speed your agenda. In fact, **you will be most effective at advancing your agenda if you let your agenda slide into the background of a genuine relationship**.

How to Take Your Performance to the Next Level

- You have an agenda. Okay. We know that about you. We get it. And we certainly value your transparency about it. But if you want us to rally around your agenda, **tie your agenda to a mission**—a purpose, a set of values, a better future, something that is bigger than you, something that can include all of us. Paint this picture for us, make it genuine, and we will make so much more happen for you.

- Yes, you can be competitive. And no, you're not a good loser—why would you ever want to become good at that? Can you now take this competitive spirit beyond a mere win-lose framework and into an outcome where both parties feel that they've won? If you put your mind to it, **you can be the architect of these win-win outcomes**. All it will take from you is the discipline of stopping for a long moment to consider the world through the eyes of the other person or team. Take the time to do this.

- **Learn to separate the small things you do to spread goodwill—the gifts, the remembered birthdays, the special favors—from the actual "ask."** People want to like you and because you are excited and exciting they want to do as you ask. But they don't want to be manipulated. To do a person a favor and then immediately make the ask: this is manipulation. To show others that you are thinking about them all the time—a note here, an interesting paper there—and then, later, a compelling challenge to act: this is true influence.

- You are an impatient person who thrills to a fast-paced, action-oriented situation. Alright. Fine. Good. We don't want to slow you down. But we do need you not to leave us behind. **So take the time to invest in a relationship with us**. Invest time in understanding our perspective, our world. You can do this as quickly and intensely as you want. But do invest this time. Otherwise we will feel as though you've fitted us into your life, when what we really want is to feel a part of your life.

- One of your most powerful qualities may well be your sense of humor. You delight in fun and irreverence. It's one of the ways you win people over. **So practice your stories, in particular the stories where you make fun of yourself**. You'll be good at it, you'll make yourself more appealing, and, of course, as a result people will be more inclined to help you get things done.

What to Watch Out For

- When you make a mistake or hurt someone's feelings (and you will; with your need to move people to act, it is inevitable), **learn to apologize**. What's wonderful about you is that mistakes and hurt feelings rarely derail you—you chalk it up to experience and then move on. What's not so great is that you've moved on so quickly that you've forgotten to be contrite. What feels like momentum to you, feels like disrespect to others. You may never do this naturally—stopping to apologize feels like stalling—so learn a couple of phrases you can say when it's clear you've pushed too hard or too fast. "How can I make this right for you?" is a good one, as is the classic, "I'm sorry."

- We live in a digital, data-based world where virtually every action and consequence can be measured. Many of the people you seek to persuade are comforted by data and are prepared to make a decision only when supplied with the data that "prove" a particular action will lead to a particular consequence. **Learn to become proficient in the language of data**. Learn how to marshal the facts so that others with a lower tolerance for ambiguity can lean on these facts and find the certainty they need.

- **Your persuasive instinct needs to be focused on the decision maker**. There's nothing worse than going all out to win someone over and persuade him to act, only to discover that he has neither the authority nor the budget to make the decision. So before you flex your influencing muscles, take the time to identify the "decider."

- Because you are energized by resistance you may sometimes, albeit unconsciously, seek out resistance simply because it is more fun to turn around a no than to get a yes right away. While it may indeed be more fun it will, of course, slow down momentum. Whenever you feel yourself being lured by the thrill of the push-back, **yank your attention back to the bigger prize of decision, action, movement, and, ultimately, impact**.

How to Win As a Leader

Influencer: Your strength is your momentum. You see, you decide, you act, you move. Us. Forward. You're on a ride, and we take the ride with you.

- You are a charismatic leader. We love to listen to you, be charmed by you, be pulled into a better future with you. We know you have an agenda. Be clear with us what it is and we'll keep letting you woo us.

- Keep your scorecards up-to-date and share them often and openly. Letting the numbers speak for themselves, simply put it out there: "We can do better than this." We will believe you.

- You are a competitor. Set up friendly but meaningful intracompany competitions to push us to give our very best. Keep the field of competition small and local. We will not only improve our performance, we will learn from our counterparts' successes too.

- You are extremely effective in getting us to commit. Just make sure we understand *why* we are committing. Take the time to explain benefits, outcomes, and the difference the change will make. Then we'll get on board.

- Your desire to "get it done now" can create errors, cause intimidation, and ultimately demotivate your most ardent followers. We don't mind being pushed, but show us you understand that there are, in fact, real time constraints.

- Learn our names. It sounds small perhaps, but you can't imagine what a difference this will make. We'll feel less like an instrument in your make-it-happen machine and more like valued contributors.

How to Win As a Manager

Influencer: Your strength is your ability to persuade me to decide, to overcome an obstacle, to act out the courage of my convictions.

- You make things happen. I love to work with someone who never loses sight of the end result. Keep reminding me of why you care so much about achieving it and how it will make a difference. Make it meaningful for me.

- You set high expectations. You push me to achieve more than I thought I could. I like to reach high, it makes the accomplishment that much more gratifying. Just please, once you've set the bar, keep it stable. A finish line that keeps moving is exhausting and demoralizing.

- Acknowledge my contributions. In a timely fashion, tell me specifically what I did that made a difference. This assures me that you're focused not only on winning but on celebrating your winners too.

- You can influence in any direction but I love to witness you managing up. You are able to clear roadblocks, get approvals, and capture the attention of the key decision makers. I know you put your neck out for us, and this motivates me to deliver.

- Set the expectations and then step out of the way. You may feel that you know the best way to do things, but let yourself be surprised by the creativity and commitment you get from your team when you let them use their own methods to achieve results.

- Trust that you made solid recruitment decisions. If someone has fallen off their game, take ownership of getting them back on track. You rarely give up on someone and they know it. Once you identify a performance issue with a team member and commit to working through it with them, they'll fight hard to get back into your good graces.

How to Win in Sales

Influencer: Your strength is your conviction. Your beliefs inspire passive clients to make a decision, to take a step, to make something happen.

- You are an activator who can't stand being idle. Your proactive drive offers incredible potential value to an entrepreneurial, start-up, or fast-growing business.

- Because you are not afraid to challenge, you can serve as a scapegoat to help me if I am the kind of client who tends to avoid conflict or ignore a problem. In taking the heat, you can call out an obvious issue, while enabling me to take action and reach a diplomatic resolution.

- To succeed in influencing me to act, help me understand the pure motives driving you. Share the source of your energy. Communicating your mission will humanize you and deepen my relationship with you.

- You will naturally set high standards for yourself and others. Define for me, your client, what excellence actually looks like—what standards are you going to meet, by when? Your specificity will spur me to act.

- Keep your message consistent. Because you've got a lot of energy and ideas, you may try different tactics to woo me, but be warned that this can confuse me (or annoy me). Your unswerving commitment to your strongest message will convince me.

- If I don't buy what you're selling at first, maintain the relationship. You worked hard to build a relationship with me; show me that our relationship is genuinely valuable to you, and next time there's an opportunity, I'll pull your card first.

How to Win in Client Service

Influencer: Your strength is that you make things happen, even if it means confronting a difficult obstacle.

- You move into action right away. Tell me what you're going to do and why you're going to do it. Your initiative immediately reassures me that my problem is not going to sit on the corner of someone's desk for two weeks.

- You want to win me over. You are very creative in how you do this and I often end up enjoying what could possibly have become an unpleasant interaction. Once you've greased the wheels with my liking you, make sure you move quickly into solving my problem. I want to like you, but I want my problem solved more.

- It doesn't surprise me that your motto is "Every client, every time." Your service is consistent, and if you can swing some additional benefit to thank me for my patience or make up for an inconvenience, you'll find it. Be creative with this and you'll stand out in my mind and my loyalty to you and your company will grow. (Be prepared: If you do this once, I will come to expect it of you! You'd better have lots of good ideas.)

- You're incredibly proactive, so show me how you can get me answers quickly. When you sense my frustration with the standard corporate reply, don't wait for me to ask to speak to your manager. Anticipate this request and go right to the top, right away. Make sure I see you do it.

- Encourage simple steps to help your team win me over. It could be as simple as telling your team to ask me "Any problems, you let us know." Or it could be a structured check-in meeting where we challenge you with "Please tell us anything and everything we could be doing differently." I will be more likely to rate my experience higher when you and your team proactively raise these questions.

- Your charm and sense of humor are engaging. Your stories are delightful. Find opportunities to connect and check in with me just because. I will be more forgiving when there's a service miss.

PIONEER

The Definition

You begin by asking, *"What's new?"* You are by nature an explorer, excited by things you haven't seen before, people you haven't yet met. Whereas others are intimidated by the unfamiliar, you are intrigued by it. It fires your curiosity and heightens your senses—you are smarter and more perceptive when you're doing something you've never done before. With ambiguity comes risk, and you welcome this.

Instinctively you know you are a resourceful person, and since you enjoy calling upon this aspect of yourself, you actively seek out situations where there is no beaten path, where it's up to you to figure out how to keep moving forward. You sense that your appetite for the unknown might be an attempt to fill a void, and some days you wonder what you are trying to prove to yourself. But mostly you leave the questioning and the analyzing to others, and revel in your pioneering nature. You are at your best when you ask a question no one has asked, try a technique no one has tried, feel an experience few have felt. We need you at your best. You lead us into undiscovered country.

You, at Your Most Powerful

- You see the world as a friendly place where good things can happen. You are not naïve, but when you think of all the possible outcomes, your mind naturally goes to the best of all possibilities. Your distinctive power starts with your optimism.

- You have a strong bias for action. You are excited to discover new things, to experience new things, and you know this will happen only if you take the first step.

- You don't neglect the need to learn and gather information—since you are an explorer at heart, you like learning new things. It's more that you believe action is the very best way to learn. What is around the next corner? The only way to know for sure is to walk around the next corner.

- Ambiguity? Uncertainty? Risk? None of these bothers you too much. You are comfortable with gaps in your knowledge, with an incomplete set of facts, because with your optimistic mind-set, you tend to fill in the gaps with positives.

- You love beginnings. At the start as you imagine where events might take you, you feel the excitement ripple through you, sharp impulses nudging, pushing, impelling you to act.

- As you move off the beaten path you are fully aware that you will meet obstacles, but for you these obstacles are part of the fun, a sure sign that you are going where none

119

have gone before you. In a strange way, they actually invigorate you.

- You move, move, move. Your life is about forward motion and momentum. As such, you are dismissive of anything that slows you down. Negative attitudes, complaining, inefficient rules or processes, you jettison all of these quickly and keep moving forward. On your journey you travel light.

- For you, new is fun. New is unknown, and the unknown challenges the status quo and shows you different avenues forward. You read deeply within and around your subject so that you can be the first to encounter new techniques, trends, and technologies.

- "Pattern interrupts" of any kind—new ideas, new goals, new projects, new people—all of these grab your attention. Can they keep your attention? Well, that's another matter.

- Other people are drawn to you because of your forward motion. You are clearly on a mission of discovery, and we want to join you on it. Who knows what we might find, and who might benefit?

How to Describe Yourself (in Interviews, Performance Reviews)

- "I love taking the first step. As long as I can remember I was this way. When I was in school . . ."

- " 'Try it and let's see what happens.' That's my motto."

- "I find I learn best when I experiment."

- "People see me as persistent. I just keep moving forward."

- "I'm one of the most resilient people I know. I bounce back fast. For example . . ."

- "I am constantly reading up on the latest research and trends. Here are a couple of things that are intriguing me right now about our business . . ."

- "I've got to say I'm a great recruiter. I can get almost anyone excited about coming on the journey with me."

How to Make an Immediate Impact

- You are not threatened by change or uncertainty, so **put yourself in the middle of it**. Seek it out. Your confidence will rise, your judgments will be sound, and you'll feel alive. For many people, the opposite is true.

- Know that you will always be an exciting—and sometimes disruptive—addition to the team. To ensure you lean more toward the exciting end of the spectrum, make sure you tie your new ideas, your new tools, and your new technologies to a problem your team is trying to solve. **Show others how your new "toy" can help them get what they want**.

- You can immediately help a team get unstuck. So to gain your team's goodwill, **seek out a roadblock they've hit** and give it the full force of your "Well, why don't we try this?" or "Have you thought about going around this way?" questions. Make sure your ideas are practical, stay with it, keep pushing to find a path of least resistance forward, and they will remember it and thank you for it.

- You are curious first, critical second. Most people are the other way around. So **lead with this open-mindedness**. When someone presents a new plan, help them run with it by asking questions and supplying them with the sort of detail that naturally occurs to you when you're thinking about the future. Do this often with your colleagues and you will come across as both calming (they won't worry that you will stamp out their fragile new idea) and inspirational (you will help them see an increasingly vivid picture of what might be).

- Because you see little benefit in "if only" thinking, you can help your new colleagues move on from past struggles or failures. Whenever they lapse into deep postmortems, **take it upon yourself to describe what good might happen the next time around**. Soon they will look to you, whether overtly or not, to redirect the team's focus forward.

How to Take Your Performance to the Next Level

- You see the "new world" and are excited by its mysteries. This makes you a potential leader of others. But remember, to get others to join you on your mission you have to describe this "new world" as vividly as you can. The more detail you give people, the more certainty they'll have, and the more likely they'll be to put aside their anxiety about the unknown and follow you. So, before you embark on your mission, **get your details together and practice your descriptions of what they will discover and how they will benefit if they sign up**.

- You have a natural instinct for change. It will serve you well to "bottle" that instinct. **Work out a formula that captures your natural instincts for how to handle uncertainty**. Turn them into a clear process that other, less risk-oriented people can follow. In your career you will meet change often. Your formula can ensure that you have a turnkey method for rallying and focusing the people around you.

- **Practice and get comfortable with a few phrases that express your natural optimism** without making you sound like a reckless fool or a naïve idealist. For example, when colleagues say, "We can't change the way we've always done it," instead of saying, "Yes we can. Just try it," ask a nonthreatening, easy-to-answer question, such as "Well, if we had *already* changed it, what would the new way look like?" This won't save you every time—some people will always be suspicious of your optimism—but by assuming that the change has already been made, it may help others break through their initial inertia.

- **Find ways to showcase how your innovations have succeeded in creating new business opportunities or new products**. These examples of how inquisitiveness turns into performance will give people more certainty, and they will become increasingly tolerant and even supportive of your pioneering spirit.

- Since you are curious first, critical second, **you could make a fantastic mentor**. You allow people to show you their best and reveal to you their dreams, and your instinct is to take the ride with them, asking one question after another, each question carrying them along a little further, a little faster. Yes, at some point, as an experienced pioneer, you should bring your critical thinking to bear on their dreams. Nonetheless, what's truly powerful about you as a mentor is your willingness to let young talent run.

What to Watch Out For

- You will always be intrigued by what's new, but you don't want to give the impression that you are simply distracted by the next shiny new object. So, to avoid this reputation while still exposing yourself to the novelty you need, **commit yourself to a disciplined schedule of "inquisitiveness."** For example, pick three great conferences a year to attend. Or once a month hold a "what's next?" roundtable, hosted by you. Or build an innovators' social community within your organization. Any one of these will a) help you feel spirited and alive, and b) give credibility and rigor to your bright-shiny-objects curiosity.

- You find it relatively easy to press the "clear" button and move on. Others don't. They struggle to let go of past struggles and find certainty—and even clarity from sift ing through these struggles and finding the lessons. You may never truly understand this kind of thinking, but it does serve some people quite well. If you work with people who need to look back before they can look forward, learn to be patient with them. **Allow them the time to sift and reflect**. If you push on before they've had this reflection time, they'll never be fully committed to your mission.

- You have more tolerance for ambiguity than most people. As such, others may mistrust your blithe reassurances about the future. These people need more from you than just "Trust me. It'll be great." First, they need a clear picture of why and how the platform they are standing on is burning—this will show them the necessity for action, now. And second, they will need a detailed description of what the platform onto which you are asking them to leap looks like and feels like. **Get good at providing people both of these pictures.**

- Possibility thinking comes so easily to you that to others it can sometimes look as though you haven't thought through all the details of what needs to be done to make the possibility real. Or worse, that you haven't appreciated how much effort it will take to execute this possibility. So, to avoid this misunderstanding, be sure to **acknowledge explicitly the time and effort required to pull off your grand scheme.** By doing this you'll appear more substantive and at the same time more considerate.

How to Win As a Leader

Pioneer: Your strength is your optimism. There are so many more ways in which things can go wrong than right. You inspire us to bet against this law of averages.

- You always have your head up, and this helps us focus. Why? Because we don't fear being blindsided (by customers, competition, the economy). Keep us informed of what you see coming next and how you plan to capitalize on it or circumvent it.

- We love that you are an adventurer, that you take risks. It's exciting for all of us to be swept along on the discovery. Paint as vivid a picture as you can of the "land of milk and honey." Help us smell the milk and taste the honey. Tell us the stories. Show us the heroes of this New World. Use as much detail and dialogue as you can when telling your stories.

- You create momentum. Put some structure around that energy. Have a daily ritual of connecting with each department for a stand-up huddle before you get caught up in the day's events. We love the opportunity to interact with you daily. The positivity you bring to these meetings, though they're brief, sets us up for the day ahead.

- Bring your sense of play to work. You have boundless creativity and imagination. Bring new games or activities to your team meetings and we'll never tire of attending. Your lighthearted playfulness is contagious and frees our own imaginations, spilling over into our interactions with our clients.

- While we love the adventurer in you, it's not always exciting to be on the expedition. Sometimes it is just plain scary. You may have undying optimism that things will work out for the best, but we need reassurance. We need to feel secure. So always share your contingency plans with us. Play out a couple of what-if scenarios.

- You are sometimes so far ahead of us that we can't even see you. Now and then stop, please. And let us catch up.

How to Win As a Manager

Pioneer: Your strength is your faith in how much further I can go. With you as my manager I keep reaching for more.

- Your optimism is infectious. I can count on you to turn my pessimism into positivity. You're not a Pollyanna; you give me concrete reasons to believe in better possibilities.

- You take risks with people. I like that you're willing to add someone with unconventional strengths to the team. I know it's because you want to push us to create something original. Just be sure you clearly explain how you see him contributing.

- Spontaneous recognition is a powerful practice to keep people engaged, and you're a master. We never know where you're going to strike next. Be specific about why you're rewarding us and we'll be sure to keep doing it.

- In our team meetings or during other activities, ensure we're matched up with people we don't normally work with. This simple step helps us connect across departments and increases our comfort in going to our counterparts when we need help during our regular workday.

- You experiment. You explore new territory. As a result, there's never a dull moment when working with you. I love this; and at times I loathe it. Everyone needs a little certainty. Pepper your pioneering with some practicality.

- You won't put up with inane processes that slow productivity. I love that you help clear the way ahead so that I can focus on getting my job done.

How to Win in Sales

Pioneer: Your strength is your resiliency. You will take risks with your clients, show them what could be, and bounce back quickly whenever you run into trouble.

- Your optimism is infectious. You see possibilities for building business when obstacles have discouraged others. Your positive view can inject hope when the team is losing faith. Substantiate the viability of your view with facts and a concrete plan to deliver.

- When barriers block your progress, you are willing to step out of your comfort zone to take a risk to win. Your willingness to experiment leads you to offer me creative solutions that your competitors may miss.

- You will tend to iterate—"Let's try this. Alright, that didn't work. Let's try this instead"—as you work to architect a solution for me. While I appreciate this constant movement forward, I will need you to define a deadline when you and I can commit to a version or approach that we are going to stick to. I do need some stability.

- Before you communicate your vision to me of what your solution will deliver, seek perspective from a practical team member to shape your message. You will be more likely to win me over when you acknowledge the potential obstacles and explain how together we can overcome them.

- Break tradition. Rather than rewarding only the leader of a top account with a gift, divvy up the budget and spend some dollars on the other people who're working hard for you. The investment of recognizing the people who're doing the work directly for you will bear immediate and lasting returns.

- Tell me true stories of how your risk-taking has paid off in the past. I need solid evidence to bring back to the decision-makers if I'm not one of them. Always give me cover.

How to Win in Client Service

Pioneer: Your strength is your confidence that things will work out.

- You start by saying, "I can solve this," which immediately allays my anxiety. Give me two concrete reasons why you are so confident.

- You are resilient. If you run into a dead end, you immediately double back and discover a new route. You just won't give up. While I appreciate your tenacity, I don't necessarily need to see it in action. Set a time and method to follow up with me. Save my time.

- You are knowledgeable. You align yourself with products that you believe will be around for the long run. Show some of your research to reassure me that I haven't invested in something that is going to be defunct in a year . . . or, if you think it is, tell me how I won't wind up looking stupid.

- You know the shortcuts. I rely on you to find the quick and easy way to get things done. Depending on the product or situation, it may be very important for me to learn the shortcut too. Ask me if I'm interested in understanding how you find and take these shortcuts.

- The effort of calling me or e-mailing me personally when your team has or hasn't met my expectations is genuinely appreciated and often unexpected. Reassure me of what you are going to do to ensure my expectations are exceeded next time around, and I'll assure you there will *be* a next time. My loyalty to your brand has a lot to do with this level of personal connection.

- Keep me abreast of changes in my industry. While I may already be aware of them, it's nice to know that someone else out there is watching out for me and wants me to be successful too.

PROVIDER

The Definition

You begin by asking, *"Is everyone okay?"* You are acutely aware of others' emotional states, particularly if you sense they are feeling hurt or slighted. You are instinctively inclusive, always looking for ways to draw others into the circle and make them feel wanted, heard, and appreciated. You pay close attention to the differences between people, each person's likes, dislikes, and foibles. *It's the only way to attend to their feelings*, you think.

You are protective of other people and will get angry or upset if you see behavior that is cavalier or dismissive of people's feelings. You are an intensely loyal and forgiving friend, but you are no pushover. Although your circle is large, it does have a perimeter and if someone's behavior offends you, you will exile them beyond the perimeter. But this exile will not last because in your heart you believe everyone can be understood, everyone can be redeemed, everyone can, in the end, be forgiven. At home and work, many will come to trust you and rely on you. You are their safe harbor, a consistently supportive presence in a world that doesn't care. And they love you for it.

You, at Your Most Powerful

- You sense other people's feelings. You feel it is your responsibility to recognize these feelings, give them a voice, and act on them.

- You are nonjudgmental and are gifted at creating a safe space in which other people's ideas and feelings can be heard. Around you, people share more because they let their guard down. Ideas, solutions, experiments—all these happen more frequently around you.

- You listen very well, and you retain the important details of the person you are listening to. And so around you, others feel heard and recognized.

- You gain other people's trust. They know that you will keep their interests in mind—and keep their confidences. *You have my back*, they think. *You will look out for me.* You are the glue that holds the team together.

- You are also the grease. Everything speeds up around you. Why? Because trust is an accelerant.

- You become a passionate defender of the perspectives of others. You may not be able to make the tough call for yourself, but so long as the "ask" is for someone else you are quite courageous. You get your strength from other people's needs and feelings and from making sure other people's needs are being met. You are at your most powerful when you do this.

- You are emotionally insightful—you see things from the other person's perspective and you know that what you see is true and valid. This means you can act on it: to change it for the better, to sell into it, to market to it, to intervene in a timely manner to avert emotionally dangerous outcomes—like a person quitting or two people clashing. All of these stem from your emotional insight.

- You have excellent institutional memory—you can retain who has been involved in an issue, what their interests were, what their emotional stake was, what their state of mind might be now.

- You are sensitive and can become defensive if you sense your perspective is not being heard.

- Because you are thin-skinned, other people can wind you up quite easily.

How to Describe Yourself (in Interviews, Performance Reviews)

- "I can pick up on other people's feelings, whether customers or colleagues."

- "People seem to trust me quickly. Why? Because I don't judge them. I find it really easy to see things from their perspective."

- "When it comes to finding solutions, I find I'm best at the brainstorming stage when people need to feel okay sharing all the ideas they have."

- "I tend to be able to remember things about people—birthdays, favorite foods, names of their kids. It makes them feel special."

- "I am an intensely loyal person. Sometimes to a fault. But I have lots of long-lasting friendships and I stand by my friends no matter what."

- "Many people in my life rely on me. And I like that."

How to Make an Immediate Impact

- **Start by taking the temperature of your team**. You have an excellent sense of the institution you are joining—as in, who is in relationship with whom, who are the heroes, what are the war stories—so feed this sense by listening and watching closely. What is said in the room? What is said only in the hallways afterward? What projects brought the best out of the team? Where does the team struggle? Who are the leaders? Who are the troublemakers?

- **Get to know the troublemakers first**, because in their minds they are misunderstood. You have a gift for allowing people to have their say and holding what they say without either criticizing it or condoning it. You just take it on. And this "taking on" lets them move out from their defensive mode and into a healthier and more productive frame of mind.

- If there are no troublemakers on the team, **start with those who need the most help**. Where are they struggling? Which aspect of their work is holding them back? How can you help them? If you're not the one to help, then can you secure the resources they need?

- As soon as you can, **assume responsibility for a specific project or task**. Obviously, you shouldn't barge your way into someone else's area of responsibility, but when a chance presents itself, volunteer to take ownership for a clearly defined deliverable. You'll get it done—because you are an instinctively responsible person—and you will begin to build your reputation as someone on whom others can rely.

- **Seek out situations that require you to listen carefully to others' concerns and secrets**. Your ability to keep people's confidences comes so naturally to you that you may take it for granted. Instead, see it for what it is—a rare quality—and put yourself in situations where it is one of the keys to success.

How to Take Your Performance to the Next Level

- **Build your base of supporters**. Who is protecting you? Who is looking out for you? You, of all people, gain strength from knowing that you are surrounded by people on whom you can rely. Amidst all the self-interest and the personal ambition, take care to build a small work "family" whom you trust utterly. You will always be at your best when you know that a few carefully chosen people have your back.

- Your need for a work family shouldn't stop you from taking on new assignments. Just know that when you move into a new position, you will sense your lack of coverage and, more than most, you will feel exposed. **Neutralize these feelings by starting to build a new "family" as quickly as you can**. Find one person you can trust, nurture that relationship, and carefully build out from there.

- Make it a ritual to gather your team together at the beginning of each week to talk about responsibilities. **Ask your people to make specific commitments**. You are at your most passionate, authentic, and persuasive when you ask people to step up and take ownership for their work.

- **Find examples of how team members supported one another and then share these examples with the team**. People often need reminding of how much they need one another, how vulnerable the "lone wolf" is, how powerful mutual support can be. Others will look to you for these vivid reminders.

- You have the potential to lead large groups of people. People will want you to lead them. They know that in you they have someone who will look out for their interests, someone who will advocate for them, someone who will expect them to step up and make a bigger contribution. **So learn how to transfer your own sense of responsibility to them**. Use stories, examples, heroes, and success stories to show them what true personal responsibility looks like in their world.

- **Seek out messy situations where trust has disappeared and conflict reigns**. Through your actions and your demeanor you can be an agent of transformation. You can serve as an example of personal responsibility and constancy. This is potentially a massive contribution to a world broken by mistrust.

What to Watch Out For

- You tend to avoid conflict when it involves you. And yet it builds and builds, until finally you explode in a way that can come as a surprise to others, in a way that can even seem irrational to others. Since you tend to fight for yourself only when you are backed into the kind of corner where your values are being questioned or challenged, **discipline yourself to use your values as backstop earlier, rather than later**. In this way you will take a stand earlier, and when it comes your stand will be, at the very least, predictable to your colleagues.

- You are not naturally politically astute. You assume that everyone will be as responsible and as inclusive as you are. And yet they aren't. And so there will be times when you are taken by surprise, times when you are disappointed by other people's blatant self-interest. **When this happens, tell yourself positive stories**. Remind yourself that though people can be selfish, they can also be trustworthy and caring and forgiving. These stories will right your ship.

- People love to share. They love to tell stories about others on the team, some of which might be quite unflattering. Resist your temptation to believe everything you hear. Before you commiserate with them, before you take on their slight and try to do something about it, **get the facts**. The slight may be imagined, and so your responsibility may be to listen to the person who is complaining and let them get it off their chest, rather than diving in and trying to right the slight. The worst reputation you can get is that you are a "gullible shoulder to cry on."

- Since you are acutely aware of personal responsibility, the sight of others whose standards of responsibility are not as high as yours will sometimes disappoint you. **Learn to move past your disappointment and into the land of expectation: "What are you going to do next time?"**

- Few are as inclusive as you are. There is always a delicate balance to be struck between people's need to be included and people's need to feel special. Often you will err on the side of including everyone and run the risk that no one will feel special. **To make everyone feel special, frame everything in the language of responsibility.** It's fine to include everyone, as long as everyone has a specific responsibility. Responsibility drives expectation and expectation drives each person's sense of self-worth. Each person feels special when something specific is expected of him or her.

- Since few are as inclusive as you are, there will be times when you are excluded. Try not to take this personally. It isn't. **It is just a function of the fact that not everyone feels your need to include everyone.**

How to Win As a Leader

Provider: Your strength is that we trust you will be there for us. You are with us. You will protect us, support us, and advocate for us. We all rely on you.

- We remain loyal to you because we know you care deeply about our experience. Guard this trust. It is your most valuable leadership asset.

- We follow you because we know you never leave anybody behind. We stay with you because of this but only because you also ensure that our strengths are being put to use in pursuit of the goal. We won't follow simply to follow—we have to feel like valued contributors. Take the time to tell us why we are special.

- Keep building your base of supporters. You need a strong, trustworthy management team around you. These people are like family to you—and this takes work to maintain. Maintain it, because with it you will be at your most powerful. Without it, you will feel surprisingly vulnerable.

- You are adaptable. If things go off plan, see the new possibilities this provides. When you demonstrate that you aren't attached to one way of doing things, you free us to call on our strengths to find the solution. This unstructured, open-minded approach supports flexibility and speed in doing what needs to be done to serve our clients.

- Whether it's a chaotic meeting, an angry client, or a mechanical mishap, tap into your talent for tenacity. Knowing that you'll stand by us and support us through the challenging parts of the day gives us the strength to push through.

- Share stories of success. You notice the wins, particularly those that involve people. Make sure we hear about them too. This will reinforce our loyalty.

How to Win As a Manager

Provider: Your strength is your unwavering support. I trust that you will never leave me dangling, exposed, and unprotected.

- I know you have my back. I can count on you to do what it takes to protect me, even if that's giving me difficult feedback about something that I need to change. You are loyal to me and so I will always be loyal to you.

- Work alongside me and catch me doing things right. You have your senses tuned to what's working, and this positive spin on managing my performance is incredibly encouraging. You don't turn a blind eye to my misses, but you frame them with "Next time, try this . . ." That tells me you want me to succeed. It works.

- You are perceptive. You pick up on the subtle energies in the room and are tactful in addressing them. You call the elephants out from under the table and sort things out then and there. I admire you for this.

- Give us leeway to choose the appropriate actions to aid a service recovery for our clients. By empowering us to make good decisions and not slowing us down by requiring us to check in with you before offering a guest a solution, we feel trusted and valued.

- Create opportunities for us to "take our work hats off" and engage in real non-work-related conversations together. Whether it's a payday luncheon or an informal off-site gathering, leverage the power of genuine connections to gel our team.

- You're sensitivity is double-edged. I can be vulnerable with you, but sometimes it's difficult for me to give you challenging feedback. I can feel your defensiveness creeping in. Counteract this by proactively seeking feedback and staying curious as to what comes up.

How to Win in Sales

Provider: Your strength is your compassion. Because you genuinely care, you act to serve the best interests of your client. Your protective nature will help clients feel secure following your counsel.

- Lead with your questions. Begin any relationship by finding out what I really need, and then make it clear that you are only selling me what I really need. From you this comes across as genuine and caring.

- If you hear me asking for something that you know isn't going to work, challenge me with your questions. Because you advise out of genuine concern, you can demand the best thinking from me with tact and grace. You help me help myself.

- Always try to get in the room with me. You feel others' emotions. Through your sensitivity, you pick up on the energy in a room and notice the subtle, nonverbal cues during a meeting.

- Your instinct is to give me a deal. This is fine—I like deals—but to save you from yourself, define in advance what your lowest limit is. Discipline yourself never to go below it or I may feel I can take advantage of you. (You might even want to bring along a partner to every meeting, someone who can hold you to this lower limit, who can save you from yourself.)

- After the initial call, allow me to be the one to follow up first. You want to begin our relationship in the manner you want it to continue, namely you listening and responding to my needs.

- If there is a product shortfall or recall, I know I will hear about it from you first. You care more about our relationship and ensuring I am set up to succeed than about defending your company. It's a relief not to have to listen to excuses. Just fix it.

How to Win in Client Service

Provider: Your strength is the sense of partnership I get from you. I know that you genuinely want me to be okay.

- You connect immediately to how I'm feeling, and you validate it. This calms me and helps me to be clear about what I'm requesting. Parrot my problem back to me so that I know you are also clear.

- If you see an opportunity to support me outside of the scope of our agreement/project, take it. You pick up on my needs and step outside the boundaries to ensure my success. I won't forget your flexibility and resourcefulness.

- You make yourself available. When I call, you find a way to pause what you're doing to help me. I have a hunch you do it for everyone, but somehow you make me feel as if I'm getting special service. This is one of your secret weapons. Sharpen it.

- I can count on you to follow up after the issue has been resolved to see if I am satisfied. You have no idea how much I appreciate this. To draw attention to it, set a time to do it and then do it at exactly that time. This sort of predictable and genuine follow-through is rare.

- Stay picky in selecting your team. You see the best in people and are more likely than others to give a break to someone who may not quite meet your standards. Be aware of this tendency. Do your interviews only with a team of people around you—they will help you keep your forgiving nature in check. And over time, they will help you maintain a reputation for attracting and retaining only the best.

STIMULATOR

The Definition

You begin by asking, *"How can I raise the energy?"* You are acutely aware of the energy in the room, and you feel compelled to do what you can to elevate it. You do this with your outlook—you are an instinctively positive person. You do this with your actions—you take a seat at the front of the room, you raise your hand to ask questions, you call upon others to contribute and volunteer. You do this with your humor—the smile in your voice.

Because you are an energy-giving person, other people are attracted to you. The world beats them down, but they know that in you they will find the power to lift themselves back up. You aren't soft and gentle. On the contrary, you challenge people to unleash their own energy, and you become impatient when someone refuses to do so, sucking energy from you and generating none of her own. But others will continue to be drawn to you because they sense that at heart you cannot help being encouraging. They sense that your natural reaction is to celebrate all that is good in them, to illuminate their strengths, and shine a light on their achievements. Even on your darkest days, you know they are right.

You, at Your Most Powerful

- You naturally focus on what is right with people, on what is going well with them.

- You are an emotional person. Sometimes these emotions take you on a roller-coaster ride, but in the end they lead you back up. Your emotional tilt is always upward.

- You derive your strength from other people. You sense their feelings and you can't help yourself: you are compelled to engage these emotions in some way and lift them up. Others call you fun, excitable, and—on your best days—inspirational.

- You are a natural host. Not of parties, necessarily—though you may be. But you are the host of other people's emotions. You feel responsible for them, for elevating them. You are an emotional turnaround expert.

- You make your presence felt. In any room, you are present, focused, a force. The meeting doesn't really start until you walk in; the energy sinks when you walk out.

- You have a magnetic quality. People's emotional bucket empties out. You, they realize, are a natural bucket-filler. And so they are drawn to you.

- You like gatherings. Since you feed off energy, the more people at a meeting or event, the more energy there is and the more energized you feel.

- "All the world's a stage" to you. You are acutely aware that other people are looking at you and are affected by you. So you pay attention to your appearance, your demeanor, how you show up in a room.

- When at an event or meeting, you pay attention to all aspects of the "show." You like picking the theme, the gifts, the colors, all the elements that can inspire people and help them have a great time. You'll dress up in the costumes. You'll take the lead in the activities. Whatever it is, there you are, ready to go at the front of the line.

- You are exuberant. You can get carried away by the emotions of the moment. When you are teaching or training or selling, or anything really, you tend to go off-script. You break free from the prescribed material and allow people to follow where their excitement and enthusiasm lead. *When people are excited they learn more, create more, achieve more*, you think. *The curriculum will just have to catch up with us.*

How to Describe Yourself (in Interviews, Performance Reviews)

- "People tell me I'm fun to be around."

- "I'm at my best when getting people excited about what they are about to do. There was this time when . . ."

- "I'm incurably positive. I believe you can find the good in virtually any situation, and I'm determined to be the one to find it."

- "Some of my best times are when I can get people together so we can rally ourselves and cheer ourselves on."

- "I think people surprise themselves by what they can achieve when they are energized. I'm the person who gets them energized."

- "I need to be out with people almost all the time."

How to Make an Immediate Impact

- You are a breath of fresh air to any team because your first response to anyone's comment or point of view is to affirm it. You nod. You smile. You encourage. **Lead with this strength**. It will encourage people to become increasingly open around you. Of course, you may not agree with everything they are telling you, but because you begin by honoring their "truth," you set things up for better collaboration in the future.

- You feed off being able to help people get what they want. So try to **put yourself in situations where you will receive immediate feedback on whether you have indeed given people what they want**. Their laughter, smiles, tears, transformations, realizations, these are your fuel. Of course, there is some risk here—maybe they won't laugh or cry or be transformed—and most people shy away from this risk. But you don't. So volunteer for this "high risk" activity and you'll not only feel more alive, you will also earn the respect of your colleagues.

- Because you present such a positive front to the world, you might initially come across as light and fluffy. To counter this, **buttress your positive energy with facts and data that support your opinions**. These will help others realize that there is substance behind the flash— "brains behind the bronze"—and, as such, you will gain much needed credibility.

- You instinctively see the best in others. So take it upon yourself to **give detailed feedback to your new team-mates**. Catch them doing something right, and then play it back for them. Tell them what you saw, why it impressed you, who benefited. You are not a fake flatterer. Instead, you are an attentive and generous audience. Your team-mates could do with more of this kind of attention—it will stimulate them to repeat their best performances.

- Your energy builds momentum toward specific outcomes. **Put yourself in situations where there are already clear goals**. Guided by these goals, your energy will have a natural channel and so will be seen as instrumental in making something happen. Target yourself in this way and you'll gain a reputation as a *productive* person, as well as a fun person.

How to Take Your Performance to the Next Level

- Over time people will come to lean on you for emotional uplift. This is a wonderful gift you offer them, and to ensure that you can keep offering it, **you must set clear boundaries for your friends and colleagues**. You cannot take on everyone's full range of emotions.

- You are skilled at handling difficult people. **Volunteer for situations where success depends on you turning around an angry or obstinate person**. It's not that you should necessarily seek out conflict—you are not, by nature, a conflict seeker. It's more that you are driven to make everything right, and so you are at your best when you have to pull out all the stops to make this happen.

- You are naturally interested in human energy of all kinds—emotional, physiological, spiritual. **Research this subject**. Depending on your personality, this could mean simply reading up on the subject. Or it could mean putting yourself through a regimen to become more proficient at managing your own levels of energy. Or it might mean watching other Stimulators in action. Whatever your preferred research style, keep looking and you will soon find some new trick, insight, or technique that will help you get better at what you do naturally.

- For most Stimulators, doing leads to learning. So keep doing. **Establish a routine where you are, with predictable frequency, putting yourself out there to gauge people's reaction**. Test whether your data, your stories, and your logic flow are landing as you hoped they would. This kind of doing-driven learning will make you more confident and certain, and to other people this reads as credible.

- **You need your "showtime."** What are the high-energy events of the week going to be? How can you give these events the attention they deserve? How can you protect them from the busy-ness of your life? How can you create more of them?

What to Watch Out For

- Just as you need your showtime, you also need your downtime. **Build into your week intentional downtime**, time when you can regenerate the energy on which so many rely. Lacking this time, you might find that you come to a point where you simply crash.

- You are good at getting people to like you precisely because you care about whether or not they like you. **Don't fight this need to be liked**—it is one of the sources of your effectiveness. Instead, seek out positions where success depends primarily on getting people to like you.

- But still, there will be times when you take things too personally. To combat this, **design a technique that will allow you to move past other people's disapproval**. This technique cannot be simply saying, "I shouldn't worry about what other people think," because you do worry about what other people think. For you, other people's energy—whether positive or negative—is tangible, physical, and while others can let it go quite easily, you are different; you are wired to hold on to it. So when you find yourself taking things personally, give yourself an emotional time-out. Walk away from the emotion of it, and instead discipline yourself to focus on the pragmatic, the practical, the "what's next?"

- In your overwhelming desire to be agreeable, it can sometimes come across to others that you have actually agreed with them, even if you haven't. Then when your true opinion emerges, the other person can feel taken aback, even "played." So, one of your biggest challenges in life will be: **How do you make your true opinions heard?** You'll never be combative, but you need to be clear. Find a technique that works for you.

How to Win As a Leader

Stimulator: Your strength is your sense of the dramatic. You are the leader who celebrates our successes, who lifts them out of the noise of experience and honors them. Your energy fuels us.

- You are our gauge for the excitement around an idea. Be hyperaware of your own energy around anything you are supporting. We will be watching your reactions.

- Our expectations are high when it comes to your story-telling. You tell vivid stories with dialogue, drama, and detail. This is an effective way to engage us, but make sure the story is real. We can smell fiction.

- Keep seeking platforms to communicate your vision. You are best face-to-face but, if that's not possible, find other unique ways to connect with us.

- Challenge yourself to make your workplace more dramatic. What can you celebrate? What can you have fun with? How about a mascot for the team? Or a nickname? Something we can all rally around. This might appear hokey to some, but you just might be able to pull it off.

- Make fun of yourself. One of your strengths as a leader is your humor. Be sure to turn it on yourself. We love seeing that.

- Find heroes within the organization and allow them to tell their own stories. Speak at staff meetings. Take pictures of excellence in action. Use video of colleagues and guests to highlight what you want to see more of. Create a quarterly newsletter. Each of these can bring excellence to life for us.

- We need to know that you'll defend us. Sometimes, in your desire to keep the emotions positive, you can come across as a bit of a yes-man or yes-woman—you can appear to agree with things you don't. Stay true to your core values and we'll continue to fight for you. And with you.

How to Win As a Manager

Stimulator: Your strength is your ability to make my work exciting. When my spirit wanes, you spark me back to give my best.

- Pay attention to the small events of my life and draw attention to them. If I buy a new car, send a gas card to my home. If I get a new kitten, send me a PetSmart gift card. If my daughter graduates from high school, give me a copy of your favorite book as a gift for her.

- Get me out of the office to visit the world of our clients. Remove us from our workplaces. Make our learning a physical experience.

- You spend more time focused on developing and leveraging my strengths than fixing my weaknesses. You seek out opportunities for me to do more of what I love, and I love you for it.

- You celebrate what's right with the world. It's inspiring to work with someone who's focused on learning from what's working rather than on criticizing and blaming. I am more encouraged to seek solutions when I know you've got this perspective.

- Your presence fills a room. If you're having a good day, everyone feels it and is buoyed by it. If not, ugh. I don't want you to be fake, though, so perhaps take a break until you've regained the spring in your step.

How to Win in Sales

Stimulator: Your strength is your enthusiasm. You bring passion and energy to clients and their projects.

- You are good in a room. Your energy, your smile, the tone of your voice—all of these are more powerful when I can actually see you. Do whatever you can to secure a face-to-face meeting with me.

- Celebrate my successes with me. Help me know what my successes are. Help me know what we should celebrate together. Help me know how.

- Your gift for creating energy stimulates me to refocus and move forward. When there is a break in momentum—and there always is—you bring the passion I need to rekindle the fire.

- You look for what's working. Your outlook is ever inspiring as you weather challenges in serving me, a (sometimes) demanding client.

- At times I may misinterpret your enthusiasm as insincere. Support your superlatives with facts so you are not viewed as a Pollyanna. And always attach your recognition and celebration to legitimate, measurable successes.

- Seek opportunities to sell in high-visibility scenarios: showrooms, trade shows, formal presentations, wherever there are lots of lights, action, and people. The stage will help you tap into your most creative and engaging self and in turn, help you sell.

How to Win in Client Service

Stimulator: Your strength is making my situation feel important. You shine a spotlight on my issue, giving me a sense that it will be taken seriously.

- You are always reaching out to me, encouraging me to be just a little more involved with the goings-on at your company than I might otherwise be. Keep doing this. I, your client, instinctively feel that there is a wall of separation between us. You excel at breaking this wall down and inviting me into your world. You put me on your "team."

- Your energy matches my energy. Rather than trying to placate me, you genuinely empathize. Just make sure it doesn't turn into a pity party. Get into action as soon as you can.

- While I value the passion you bring to my problem, at times it will serve us both better if you display the opposite emotion from mine. If my voice gets louder, yours gets softer. If I talk faster, you talk slower. This can help balance what could be an overreaction on my part.

- You maintain your intensity throughout the process of solving my issue. You seem tireless. I love to have someone working so hard for me. Use your humor to diffuse the tension if it gets too thick.

- Use your energy to light a fire under your colleagues. If someone else needs to be engaged to help me, motivate him to move at the same speed as you. I love it when I feel that there is an entire team mobilized to help me; and you, of all people, are a fantastic mobilizer.

- In your effort to keep me happy, you may find yourself agreeing to measures that you cannot in fact take. It will be worse to have to renege on a commitment, so be realistic about your service recovery. Make as few promises as possible and keep them all.

TEACHER

The Definition

You begin by asking, *"What can he learn from this?"* Your focus is instinctively toward the other person. Not his feelings, necessarily, but his understanding, his skills, and his performance. You see each person as a work in progress, and you are comfortable with this messiness. You don't expect him to be perfect; in fact, you don't want him to be perfect. You see the possibility in imperfection. You know that imperfection creates choice, and that choice leads to learning.

Since you are energized by another person's growth, you look for signs of it. *Where was he last month?* you ask yourself. *What measurable progress have I seen?* You create novel ways to keep track of his performance and celebrate with him when he reaches new heights. You ask him a lot of questions to figure out what he knows and what he doesn't, how he learns best, what is important to him, and what journey he is on. Only then can you join him at the appropriate level and in the appropriate way. Only then can you help him learn.

You, at Your Most Powerful

- People's performance improves when you're around. This is your greatest gift.

- Instinctively people know that you care about them and that your caring is genuine. They get it. They feel it. They never doubt it. And this certainty frees them. They can experiment and reach and fall and fail, and then reach again. And you will still be there willing them to keep reaching.

- You don't give up on people. No matter how much they struggle, you keep believing that they will find a way to move forward and to improve.

- You are intrigued by the process—the process of other people's learning and growth. You aren't impatiently waiting for the big-bang breakthrough. Instead you are content to see small increments of growth that happen every day. The "getting it" can be more exciting to you than the "got it."

- The other process that intrigues you is the process of the activity. You revel in breaking activities down into their discrete parts and then showing others how to do each discrete part. You want others to understand the "how"— the "method"—and when you can show others the "how" you are delighted. This, in your view, is where the real learning happens.

- You give other people choices. You allow them to make their own decisions. You realize that choice is the mechanism for learning, for growth. You say, "You decide, then come back and tell me what you decided, and why." You are a natural delegator.

- You know that people can learn only from where they are starting, so you ask lots of questions to determine their starting point. You listen very carefully. You watch closely. Any small action or reaction could be a clue as to where to join them in their learning journey.

- For others, this "start-by-listening" approach makes them feel heard and safe. For you it is the source of vital information about their learning styles, their personality, their understanding. You use this information to tailor what you are teaching so that it fits each person—you individualize.

- Physically you want to get on people's level. You want to "walk the factory floor," see people in their "natural habitat," "get down in the dirt with them." This achieves three things: 1) it shows them that you know them; 2) it shows you the world from their perspective; 3) it gives you the raw material you need to give them good ideas for how to get better.

- You are a learner yourself. Because you love the process of "getting it" you sign yourself up for classes so that you can feel yourself "getting it." This is a constant part of your life.

- Your constant learning is not just for your benefit. It also serves to arm you with new ideas and techniques that you can use to help others. Consequently, to others you seem wise, an unending source of knowledge, experiments, and ideas that might help them grow.

- Whenever others run dry—of ideas or of self-belief—they return to you. You seem strong, patient, understanding, and yet always expectant.

How to Describe Yourself (in Interviews, Performance Reviews)

- "I like listening to people tell me what they do and how they do it."

- "I'm a constant learner. For me there's something energizing about the process of getting to a point where I've mastered a new skill. Recently I took classes to learn how to . . ."

- "I like getting down in the dirt with people, seeing the world through their eyes. Customers, colleagues, friends— I think I can truly help them only if I have seen their perspective."

- "I don't think you can teach all people in the same way. Instead I'm always looking for how each person's mind works, and what motivates them."

- "I never give up on anyone. In my heart I know that everyone can find success somewhere—we just have to persevere with them and discover where. Of course, it might not be within their current position."

- "I love giving my people ideas; I'm constantly reading up on stuff so that I've got something to share with them when they call on me."

- "I get a kick out of sharing my ideas or techniques with my colleagues. Knowledge is one of those weird things where you get more of it by giving it away."

How to Make an Immediate Impact

- You want to help others, but you have to earn this right. So **begin with your student hat on**. People like students. They like to be asked questions about how they do what they do, and they like to hear themselves talk about why it works. Listening shows respect. So be inquisitive and be seen to be inquisitive.

- **Find opportunities to feed people's words back to them**. Describe what you've heard and what you've come to understand about their work and their process. Not only will you be able to test your understanding, you will also validate your new colleagues. They will appreciate this validation.

- **"Sweep the floors" with your new colleagues**. Spend time with them in their environment. Watch how they do their work and notice the details of their struggles and their successes. These real-world details will give you raw material when you start trying to help them navigate through their struggles and achieve even greater success.

- Early in your new position, **find a chance to expose your team to at least one new idea**. Since you are constantly studying, reading, and researching, you will doubtless have new ideas to share. And since you have shown yourself willing to listen and learn, you will have earned the right to offer your colleagues a fresh perspective. Pick one idea in which you have great confidence and present it to the team.

- **Volunteer to teach**. Teams are busy doing, and yet they know that new additions to the team will need to be brought up to speed. Some are frustrated by the novice's lack of knowledge, but you aren't. You are excited by their "ignorance." Each novice is a chance to find interesting ways to fill in the gaps in his or her knowledge.

- Having asked your questions and "swept the floor" with your colleagues, **offer a way to help people track their progress**. Because you are interested in improvement, you will be adept at figuring out how to help people measure what they do; or, if measurement proves too complicated, how to define increasing levels of competency at a particular skill or task. Since everyone loves to chart their progress toward mastery, this could be an invaluable and immediate contribution.

How to Take Your Performance to the Next Level

- **Keep learning**. Keep researching your subject. Attend the cutting-edge conferences. Read the expert posts. Make this a priority.

- **Become an overt champion of others**. Discipline yourself to reach across the organization and place people whose raw talent you have spotted into positions of real responsibility. Some will say, "But she is not ready." Don't shy away from this risk. Instead, celebrate it. You are a genius at giving people just the kind of responsibility they need, at just the time when they need it.

- When you champion young talent in this way, **make sure your explanations for why this is the right person, the right responsibility, and the right time are vivid and detailed**. Become adept at describing the strengths you have seen in the person and why you think this strength will translate to the new, larger responsibility. Be equally detailed about what specific knowledge the person lacks, and how you propose this person go about acquiring this knowledge, without jeopardizing their ability to deliver results. This detail will give others, who have less of a feel for young talent, the certainty they need.

- **Develop theory**. As an instinctive collector of factual bric-a-brac, you will always be a fount of new ideas and insights. But if you want to excel at helping others learn, you need a set of theories on which to hang all that your inquisitiveness has yielded. Theories clarify. They help others make sense of things. And so they will make you a better delegator.

- **Refine your stories.** People are wired to be interested in a story that has a beginning, a middle, and an end. They love the momentum, the drama, the detail, and the dialogue of a good story. Since you excel at noticing detail, and since you love the drama of learning and discovery, you will always have rich raw material from which to construct your stories. Take the time to do so. It will make you a better teacher.

- **Always stay in touch with those whom you have helped to learn and grow.** Their continued success will be a constant source of joy for you. They are your alumni.

- **Build your network of other "teachers."** They will invigorate you with their ideas, their practical approaches, and their successes. They will push you to stay on top of new developments and to keep innovating.

What to Watch Out For

- **Stay in the real world**. Trust the details you notice. You are such an avid reader and researcher you can sometimes be intrigued and even swayed by other people's theories. While some of these theories may be sound, always rely on your own real-world learning as your guide.

- **Know that things will not always work out as you had hoped**. A new young talent whom you championed will struggle. A new idea that you introduced and supported will fail to take hold. Be resilient and keep confident in your process, namely, that in most cases experimentation and delegation lead to progress.

- Teachers can sometimes come across as know-it-alls, so **guard your credibility**. This means a) keep doing your real-world research so that you always have on hand two or three recent examples of what you've seen and the sense you've made of it; and b) learn to be comfortable saying, "I don't know and I will get back to you with the answer as soon as I can." Never pretend to know what you don't.

- It will be hard for you to thrive without an audience, even if your audience is a readership rather than a group of people you actually know. **So seek out your audience of learners and resist the temptation to get yourself promoted too far away from them**.

- When you join a new team, the learner aspect of you will do battle with the teacher aspect. The teacher aspect will immediately see people who could improve and ideas that could be spread. **Hold this teacher aspect in check.** You can't simply waltz into a new setting and proffer advice and wisdom—well, you can, but it will be badly received. So in the learner-teacher battle, let the learner win. Ask your questions, take notes, be known for listening, and your wisdom will be more appreciated and more readily adopted.

How to Win As a Leader

Teacher: Your strength is your faith in our potential. We never sense frustration with our struggles but rather sense a deep belief that we can keep experimenting and keep getting better. You accept us; and yet your expectations motivate us.

- We want to learn from you. And you want to teach us. So make time to teach us. Set aside one lunch a week to walk us through what you have learned along the way. Volunteer to be faculty for a series of classes. Blog about your experiences.

- You take the time to understand things from our perspective, and we love you for it. You are in touch with people's everyday experience. Keep finding ways to demonstrate that this remains important to you. Stay "on the floor" with us. Keep yourself as close as possible to where the real decisions are made.

- Keep our core score visible and up-to-date. Knowing that you are monitoring our progress is motivating. You always find unique ways to celebrate our personal and organizational successes.

- Lead with your questions. You are one of those leaders who don't believe that they have all the answers. Instead you look to us for the answers. Set up a regular coffee or lunch with us where you ask us what we think we can do to make the team perform better.

- You value experimentation and hands-on experience. This drives us. We know that it's okay to make mistakes. We will soon appreciate that you expect us to articulate what we learned from those mistakes and thereby increase our organizational wisdom. Make this a definitive aspect of your leadership.

How to Win As a Manager

Teacher: Your strength is how seriously you take my learning. And since you take it so seriously, since you pay it so much attention, I am inspired to do the same.

- You make yourself available. I never feel as if I'm intruding or taking too much of your time. You seem genuinely to perk up when I enter your office to ask for guidance or insight.

- I actually look forward to my performance reviews with you. I know you've actively monitored my progress, and I know that you'll be creative in finding ways to help me elevate my performance to the next level.

- You reward with opportunity. If I've achieved something important, I can count on you to present me with a special project or mission to augment my skills. This focus on my growth shows me that you really care about my long-term development and ultimately, fulfillment.

- You individualize. I know that you support each of us differently, teach and reward us in distinct ways, and I don't mind. I see the collective difference that it makes. Find obvious opportunities, such as a potluck lunch where we all have to bring in our favorite dish, for me to reveal more of who I am.

How to Win in Sales

Teacher: Your strength is your understanding. Your rich perspective of how each client is unique enables you to adapt your offering to serve them better.

- Give me all your numbers. Tell me I can call you at any time, for any reason. You put the priorities of others above your own. You need to feel needed. This prompts you to drop everything to answer a question or explain an offering. Through your genuine attention, you make me feel important and valued.

- One of your gifts in sales is that you don't need to have all the answers. You want to tell me what you know and then allow me to draw my own conclusions. I admire and appreciate this.

- As a Teacher you are also a natural learner. Learn from me. Ask me to share what I know. Let me speak about my world. I will sense that you are genuinely intrigued and so I will be drawn to you.

- You win through a highly individualized sales approach. As such, you will naturally thrive in sales positions where you don't lead with your product, but instead where you have to evaluate thoroughly my need and then piece together a customized offering. The more that customization is the key to success, the more successful you will be.

- While your sales style fosters lasting business relationships, at times you may find that your approach requires a longer sales cycle to close. You may want to partner with an Influencer to initiate a new sales relationship or, failing this, focus on positions that support a longer sales cycle.

- You thrill in demonstrating all the cool features of the product. I can tell that you're not simply going through the motions but that you're genuinely committed to ensuring that I learn all the different ways the product can help me. Just notice when your enthusiasm has outlasted my interest.

How to Win in Client Service

Teacher: Your strength is that you help me discover something new about my situation.

- Always seek to find opportunities to teach me. Say, "You're using X, but Y will work better for you. Here's why . . ."

- If there is a shortcut or a work-around for an issue I'm having, show it to me. When you have advice on how I might use my product or service more effectively or efficiently, share it. This learning breeds loyalty.

- Ask lots of questions to discover my level of expertise with the product, and then teach from there. Reassure me that whatever knowledge I have is a perfectly good place to start. This will keep me from feeling naïve.

- Give me an opportunity to show my knowledge. I'm more apt to listen and learn once you've acknowledged my expertise.

- Share your expertise regularly. Look for ways to stay in contact with me, to inform me of product changes, new offerings, and opportunities to learn more about what I've purchased from you. A monthly newsletter, or a weekly blog, for example.

- You leave me feeling as if I'm better off after interacting with you. I am more knowledgeable and more confident. Most importantly, I know I have a trusted resource to call if I run into future issues.

CHAPTER 4

The Three Strengths Principles

How to Build Your Strengths for a Lifetime

Even with the help of tools such as StandOut it can be quite the challenge to build your strengths for a lifetime.

Sure, you have innate genius. Everybody does. This word "genius" might strike you as a bit overblown, but only because *genius* gets tossed around pretty cavalierly these days. Everyone from the latest disposable pop star to a chef who knows how to make *crème brulée* is dubbed with the term. In fact, if you do a search for "Marcus Buckingham is a genius," you'll get . . . well, you won't get any hits at all. But let's not dwell on that. What I'm getting at is simply that the word *genius* has become diluted and has evolved, as many words do, quite far from its original meaning.

Genius derives from the Latin *gignere*, meaning "to beget," and its original sense in English described a guardian spirit present with a person from birth—something like a guardian angel. Many of us in the twenty-first century may not think a lot about guardian spirits, but the word changed over time to take on the broader sense of a person's natural, inherited abilities. And in this sense, we do all have a genius.

I've seen it in my own kids. Okay, I didn't actually see any spirits hovering over my daughter Lilia when she was born, but I have seen her genius in action literally from her first words. Lilia started talking later than most children do, but when she did start, she spoke in complete sentences. One of her first utterances, as she lay there, a sweet-natured, wide-eyed, three-year-old, looking up at her mom, was this: "Mommy, that's a lovely necklace."

Of all the possible sentences she could have picked, why did she pick that one? No simple "More!" or "Stop!" for her, no sir. She chose to compliment her mother's accessories. And I think I know why.

You might expect me to say that she went on to become a child prodigy fashion designer, or that she was reading at a fifth-grade level in the first grade. Well, I suppose Lilia is as interested in clothes as any young girl, but she doesn't have any designs ready to show in Milan. And I think she's plenty bright, but it's not as if she's already parsing Shakespearean iambic pentameters in kindergarten.

No, what Lilia was showing us with that first sentence was a precocious tendency toward something psychologists call "reciprocal altruism." That is to say, she was aware that good-will is harvestable: if you sow it now, you may be able to reap it in the future. So when she complimented Mommy on her neck-lace, she realized that by saying something nice right now, later on Mommy might be nice to her in return. We didn't teach her this—and if she didn't possess it, I have no idea how we would. Lilia just instinctively understands reciprocal altruism, and she uses it to get people to do what she wants them to do.

That may sound cynical on her part, but the thing is, Lilia doesn't *know* she's doing it. She just does it, naturally. It's part of her genius. And in ways far beyond her conscious understanding it guides her actions and pushes her to do things that most other kids don't. At school, for example, Lilia has deployed this genius to finagle her way into her schoolmates' hearts. What should be a twenty-second walk from the assembly hall to her classroom routinely takes ten minutes as fourth, fifth, and sixth graders, who shouldn't even know she exists, scoop her up into a smoochy "Lilia!" hug, as she squeals with delight. After being at the school only a couple of months, she'd already been sowing goodwill. She can't stop herself.

At her most recent parent-teacher conference, Lilia's teacher showed us the results of a class project in which the children had set goals for the upcoming semester (excellent training for the future denizens of corporate America). The first goal seemed worthy enough: "Learn to write better" (misspelled). All right, that's to do with knowledge. We can work on that. No real worries here. Move along to the next one.

The second goal was more alarming: "Stop fooling the teachers." Excuse me? Stop fooling the teachers? Since when do children this young have to be reminded not to manipulate their teachers? Have I missed something? Maybe it's a generational thing? Perhaps many of the other children had that on their list of goals as well? How many—ah, none. Okay, then. Apparently our child is unique.

If I needed confirmation that not every child approaches life the same way Lilia does, I got it that night from my son, Jack. I shared the story of Lilia's goals with him—*mea culpa*. Not the wisest parenting move, I now realize, expecting him to chuckle with me when I got to the "stop fooling the teachers" part. There were no chuckles. Not even a grin.

"You can fool the teachers?" he asked, baffled.

"Er, no," I fumbled. "I just meant that . . ." I stopped. I could see I'd lost him. He was trying to recalibrate his understanding of a universe in which teachers could actually be fooled. His confusion was less "*How* do you do that?" than "*Why* would you even want to do that?"

Such behavior in my five-year-old is amusing, even kind of adorable. But you can see how this same genius for reciprocal altruism that makes her schoolmates love her might get her into trouble down the line. She's not too young to *have* this genius, but she's still too young to channel it intentionally and put it to good use. She could turn out to be very effective at influencing people in sales, say, or as a leader. But if she's not conscious and careful about what she's doing, she could easily squander this gift and turn into a manipulative person.

Of course, one would hope that we adults are all conscious and intentional enough that we recognize our genius for what it is, and channel it appropriately.

But what if we're not?

What if we're all, when it comes to our genius, our unique combination of strengths, the equivalent of five-year-olds—using our genius, if at all, haphazardly and without any real sense of purpose and direction?

Obviously I don't mean to compare you to a five-year-old. My point is simply that despite the fact that your genius—your particular combination of strengths—is deeply a part of who you are, it is exceedingly challenging to understand it, take control of it, and make it work for you.

The most basic challenge, of course, is that it's hard to see your own uniqueness. As I saw with Lilia, your strengths are a part of you whether you're conscious of them or not. And because they're so woven into the fabric of who you are, they can actually be quite difficult to pinpoint. Certain things come so naturally to you that you don't see your ability to do them as unique; you just think it's you. Or rather, you don't even think anything. You just do what you do because it comes to you too easily to require any analysis. It's not that you don't value your uniqueness; it's that you don't *see* it. You may even assume that your abilities are no big deal because everybody must have them.

Which points to a second challenge: other people don't care what makes you unique. As oblivious as we can be to our own strengths, it's even easier to ignore the particular and unique strengths of others. We assume that if we have a talent or inherent ability, everybody else does too. Or if we're not naturally drawn to doing something, we find it hard to understand why anybody else would be.

No one else is worrying about what makes you unique. Nobody is dedicated to identifying that special cluster of talents you have. School doesn't do it—they want to make sure that everybody learns what everybody is supposed to learn. Work doesn't do it—they're most concerned about what needs to get done. Everybody in your life has expectations and demands that don't necessarily have any direct connection to your strengths. It makes for a lot of background noise.

If you were an engineer, you might say that your life has a terrible signal-to-noise ratio. Even if you felt impelled to ask yourself, "What is my genius? What am I drawn to do naturally? What makes me who I am?" you are surrounded by crowds of people advising you to "try this" and "you have to do it this way" and "be like that," drowning out that impulse.

Though your genius is ingrained, the right way to channel it is not. This final challenge is that even if you do cut through the noise and identify what unique strengths you have to offer, that's still not enough. To be truly your best, it isn't sufficient merely to understand *that* you're unique or even to understand what *makes* you unique. Sustained success comes only when you take what's unique about you and figure out how to make it *useful.*

Your strengths, in essence, are value-neutral. They can be put to good use, or they can (as Lilia's poor teachers can attest) be put to bad use. If you don't own your strengths, if you don't know them and understand them and consciously decide how you can best apply them in your life, they *will* come out anyway. But you won't be in control of how they do.

On your own personal strengths journey, here are three principles to guide you:

Principle #1: Your Genius Is Precise

Current thinking about effectiveness advises us to be flexible, versatile quick-studiers, ready-willing-and-able to jump from one challenge to another. A close scrutiny of excellence, however, reveals that our edge—our particular genius—is quite precise. We each have specific areas where we consistently stand out, where we can do things, see things, understand things, and learn things better and faster than ten thousand other people can. And when we find ourselves in these areas, our "strengths zone" if you will, we are magnificent. Self-assured and flushed with success, we imagine we can do just about anything that we turn our minds to.

And yet we can't. Move us even slightly out of our strengths zone, and our outstanding performance falls to average alarmingly quickly.

Michael Jordan offers an extreme example. As foolhardy as it now seems in retrospect, Jordan retired from the NBA in his prime to attempt to do in baseball what he had already accomplished in basketball. Jordan had been a high school baseball all-star, and, although he opted for basketball in college, it remained a lifelong dream of his and his father's to be a professional baseball player. After his dad's untimely death he felt compelled to honor the dream they had shared. When he first started out, Jordan hit .202 in the minor leagues (barely above the fabled "Mendoza Line" of .200 that baseball fans refer to as the minimum competence for a hitter at any level). But his work ethic in basketball was legendary, and he applied the same dedication to his baseball career. In just one year, he raised his average to .252.

A 50-point year-to-year increase in batting average is remarkable in any league. Terry Francona, his manager at the time (and current manager of the Boston Red Sox) claims that with a little more work, Jordan could well have made it to the big leagues—and furthermore, Francona insists that there the legendary Michael Jordan would have been . . . a journeyman player. At best. And if that's all he'd ever done, you'd never have heard of him.

After one season in the minors, Jordan returned to the Chicago Bulls to win three more NBA Championships. He was not the same player he was before—not according to his coach Phil Jackson. According to Jackson he was a better player, more passionate about the game, more in control of his gifts, and, significantly, much more inclusive of his teammates.

His time away from basketball had taught him not that career experiments are useless—during his time with the Birmingham Barons he discovered a great deal about the extent and the limits of his own strengths, as you will if you decide on what turns out to be a misguided career detour. Rather, what he learned is that you have to fully own your own genius before you can responsibly offer it up to others.

Michael Jordan is a distant figure, both in level of achievement and, now, in years since he last graced the basketball court. I saw the precision of genius much closer to home. At a very early age my sister, Pippa, discovered that she could dance—not just move in time to the music, but dance as though her guardian angel had been teaching her for centuries. She donned her tutu, skipped off to ballet class every afternoon, and then, at thirteen, attended the Royal Ballet Boarding School where years of bar work and choreography and movement classes prepared her to graduate into the Royal Ballet Company itself and become the perfect classical English ballet dancer.

The problem for Pippa was that the "perfect classical English ballet dancer," the dancer who could take the lead role in *Swan Lake* or the *Nutcracker*, was supposed to be a brilliant technical athlete. She was supposed to be able to do four pirouettes to the left and four to the right, and then do it again and again, without breaking a sweat. And Pippa couldn't. She could do three—no problem, three to the left and three to the right—but not four. More than ten thousand hours of deliberate practice, huge talent, unbelievable dedication, but still she couldn't do what was needed to excel in her chosen field. At this point it looked as if she'd never become a principal dancer. It looked as if she'd picked the wrong career.

But she hadn't. Her career didn't stall. During her years in school, Pippa had discovered that she wasn't just a "dancer." Instead she was a dancer with a particular set of strengths. She was a lyrical dancer, a dancer of beautiful lines, flowing form, long legs, and the most expressive arms you'd ever seen. And so when she realized that she would never excel in the ballet company she had dedicated her life to, she wasn't utterly derailed. Instead, she thought deeply about the precise nature of her "genius" as a dancer, and then sought out a very particular dance company, the Nederlands Dans Theatre, which specialized in making dance pieces for lyrical dancers, dancers whose strength was grace rather than pure athleticism. After a couple of nerve-racking auditions, she was hired by the company and then spent the next ten years— ten wonderful, challenging, highly successful years—expressing her unique strengths in dance.

No matter where you look, you can find examples of how surprisingly precise genius is. Ellen DeGeneres is a stellar entertainer? Well, no. Ellen is a gifted comedienne, but move her even slightly off her game and put her behind the judges' desk of *American Idol* and her brilliance fades. Likewise, Jon Stewart is a funny, ironic, and always winning host. Well, yes . . . of his own political commentary show. Ask him to host the Oscars and his irony translates as condescension, so the jokes aren't funny and the audience is lost.

Robert Nardelli, president of GE's Power Systems division, is a genius-level leader, and leadership is transferable, right? Not necessarily. Install him as CEO of Home Depot or Chrysler and he doesn't look quite so impressive.

As CEO of Hearst, Cathy Black was the modern-day model of the modern media executive, versatile, plugged in, focused, and efficient. Upon her retirement, she was appointed superintendent of New York City Schools. She flamed out after three months.

Malcolm Gladwell is a phenomenal writer, and since writing is writing, shouldn't his skill be transferable from articles to books? Not exactly. His true genius is the carefully argued, silky-prosed, three-thousand-word article—today there is no one better. But when he comes to write his books, this genius accompanies him, he can't shake it, and so his books all have the same recognizable quality: a series of elegant articles wrapped around a common theme.

Your genius will be similarly precise. This doesn't mean you shouldn't experiment with new positions or stretch yourself with new challenges, as Gladwell did in moving from articles to books. You should. But when you do, know that, consciously or not, you will bring your particular brand of genius with you.

This means that if you want to become, let's say, a manager, you won't be able to be just any sort of manager. On the contrary, your genius as a manager will depend on the specific strengths you possess. Similarly, if you put yourself in a leadership position, you will be a very particular kind of leader. If you are in client service, you will excel in a distinct way.

For example, imagine that the StandOut assessment reveals your top two strengths Roles as Influencer and Pioneer. This is what your results say about the competitive advantage you will bring to any position, any team:

You keep innovation high on the agenda, challenging us to make the exceptional real. You are usually the first on the block to own the newest toy or gadget and you love to tell the stories of how you got it, how it works, how it's going to revolutionize . . . everything. As soon as everyone starts buying what you're selling, however, you're on the waiting list for version 2.0. You revel in introducing ideas that create a furl in people's brow. If you see a skeptical, quizzical look in their eyes, you know you've hooked one. You don't like to rally behind anything obvious or conventional. If everyone else is doing it, it pains you to tow that line. In fact, you will swim against the tide for the simple joy of seeing if you can get anyone to swim with you.

Apply these characteristics to a manager position and you will be the kind of manager who challenges, cajoles, persuades, is never satisfied, pushing for more, pressing for action. It will always be an intense experience working directly for you. But whether this intensity comes across to us, your employees, as invigorating or as exhausting depends on how good a job you do at understanding and channeling your genius.

As a leader your style will be characterized by optimism about the future and an impatience to get us there. Your sense of momentum is acute, visceral. It will define you as a leader. But, again, whether this translates to us, your followers, as a dynamism from which we can all draw energy or as mere recklessness will depend on how well you focus it.

In a service role your power will be your confidence that things will work out right. You will confront any obstacles and root out any shortcut to make things right for me, your client. You cannot *not* be this sort of service provider. Whether this winds up making me, your client, happy in the long run, however, isn't certain. You could become a blowhard who promises more than he can deliver. Or, with your strengths sharp and focused, you could excel as the first line of defense for difficult clients needing help with novel, as yet untested, products.

In each of these positions you *can* excel, as you can in many others. But you are most likely to do so only when you understand and respect how precise your genius truly is.

Which, of course, leads to the next principle.

Principle #2: You Can't Respect What You Don't Remember

In a world that doesn't really care about you and your strengths, the responsibility falls to you to apply your strengths *consciously* every day. Ironically, the unconscious nature of strengths—the fact that you are most yourself when you vanish into whatever you are doing—makes this quite difficult to do. And yet, if you don't do it, if you allow your strengths to remain as unconscious, subliminal reactions, you won't have a lifeline to grab on to when events conspire to yank, lull, or lure you off your strengths path.

After college Michael became a software engineer, writing code. And because he was good at it and hardworking and reliable, he got promoted to team leader. Here he also excelled. He is a wonderful explainer. Some people get impatient when new team members don't understand something. Not Michael. For some reason the more difficulty a person has in understanding something, the more patient he becomes. He slows right down to their speed and walks them through what they need to "get," step by step. (In the language of StandOut, his top two strength Roles are Teacher and Equalizer.)

His team loved him. And so he was promoted again, this time to project manager.

Now he was being paid to run an entire project for his company, and the strengths required were very different from the team leader position. The two most important were first, designing-testing-redesigning the software as the project went along (Pioneer), and second, handling the client warmly and tactfully (Provider).

Michael struggled with both. He hated it when the software didn't do what it was supposed to do, and then having the client see it not do what it was supposed to do, and then having to charm his way through the meeting so that the client wouldn't feel panicked, and then having to repeat the whole horrible process at the next update meeting. Each time the software wouldn't do something it was supposed to, and each time he would have to find the right way to dance around it and put the client at ease.

This might not sound like hell to you. You might embrace the inherent ambiguity in this kind of design-and-hand-hold-as-you-go position. But Michael didn't. He was *capable* of it—he's smart and reliable and hardworking—but it drained him. Day by day it dragged him down, slower and slower, until one day he stopped altogether. In his words: "One morning I just couldn't put my key in the car door."

That day was fifteen years ago. And he hasn't worked since.

They say that burnout happens the same way that bankruptcy does: gradually, gradually, then suddenly. This was certainly true for Michael. In the project manager position, he found himself day after day being asked to have strengths he didn't have. He became weaker and weaker, until suddenly one day he broke down. That day is where he is today. Fifteen years have gone by, and though he has fought hard—harder than I think I might have done if my life had emptied me out—he hasn't moved.

I was talking to him the other day and for the first time in a long time he brought up that day when everything stopped.

"I just didn't have it, Marcus. I didn't have what it took to get the job done. I knew it. My boss knew it. Everyone knew it."

"Well, what did you used to be good at?" I asked quietly. "When you used to look forward to going to work, which activities did you look forward to?"

At first he said nothing. He just sat back on his sofa staring up at the ceiling, and I thought he'd ignored me or couldn't be bothered to answer. Then, with a small smile, he looked at me and said: "Tutorials. I was really good at writing tutorials. I loved trying to pretend I was looking at a computer screen for the first time and had no idea what to do, what button to press, what sequence to follow. I loved doing that. I loved writing really helpful tutorials."

It was such a weirdly precise thing to say, and yet he said it as if he'd never known it before that moment. He certainly hadn't known it fifteen years ago. Or at least he hadn't known it clearly enough. When he started to struggle, when "everyone knew" that he didn't have what it took to succeed in his new position, he had no conscious strengths to fall back on. He came to believe what everyone around him was telling him, that he didn't have what it took to get the job done, and gradually—then suddenly—his confidence disappeared. And one day he couldn't put the key in the car door and drive to work.

Obviously I'm not saying what happened to Michael will happen to you. I *am* saying that life will throw obstacles at you. Take responsibility now for remembering what your core strengths are so that you can grab on tightly to them when things go awry. When you take a job you should never have taken, when your boss doesn't understand you, when your company RIFs you, when you start to question whether you have anything of value to offer, understanding your strengths will hold you in place, reorient you, and show you the way forward.

All that to say one of the most important outcomes from taking the StandOut assessment is simply that you remember your results. This is why we've chosen to target only your top two strength Roles. We could keep cutting these Roles into ever-thinner slices, or drill down into your third, fourth, and fifth Roles, but what we would gain in complexity we would lose in practicality—a week after taking the test you wouldn't be able to recall what your strengths were, and since what you can't recall you can't consciously apply, much of StandOut's power would slip away.

When I took StandOut, my top two were Creator-Stimulator. If you want to know what this says about me, by all means turn to page 204–205, but, frankly, at the most basic level, what matters is that I remember those two words. If I can remember those two words for a week, then I am more likely to think consciously about how I am using those strengths that week. And if I can do this for one week, my brain's retrieval of those two words will become just that little bit easier, and so I am more likely to be conscious of how I am applying them the next week, and the next, until ten years from now, if you ask me what my StandOut results were, my memory paths would be so well worn—technically, the memory would have migrated from the hippocampus, where all midterm memories are stored, to the cortex, where long-term memories live—that they would be instantly accessible to me.

To beat life's terrible signal-to-noise ratio, you are going to have to turn up the signal. And the best way to do that is repetition. So keep it simple. Take StandOut, remember your top two Roles, think about how you're going to channel them today, and then do the same again tomorrow. And tomorrow.

Principle #3: You Must Reach Beyond Your Roles

Conventional wisdom tells you to push yourself beyond your comfort zone. Yet when you study the most successful people you discover that they do something quite different: they push themselves *within* their strengths zone. They certainly aren't complacent. It's more that they realize they will be at their most productive, their most creative, their most generous, their most collaborative if having found their edge, they spend their life sharpening it.

How do they do this? By using the raw material of their life to add detail to their understanding of their strengths. As I mentioned, my top two strength Roles are Creator-Stimulator. Since there are seventy-two different permutations of top two strengths

Roles, it is possible that you have the same combination. And if you do, you and I will have much in common. We will both be enthusiasts, always looking to bring energy and optimism to new ideas. We will both be at our best when we know our subjects deeply, when we have crafted stories about our ideas, and when we have tailored our stories to each of our "audiences." Yes, we will have to watch out that we don't throw our full force behind an idea before we have vetted it fully, but, on our best days, both of us will be a compelling and uplifting force to our friends, colleagues, and families.

And yet there the similarities might end. The content of your ideas, the way in which you present them to others, how you dramatize them, and indeed your ultimate reasons for doing so, will almost certainly be different from mine.

To sharpen your edge, use your top two Roles as a starting point for investigating what your strengths look like in the real world. To help you begin, try an exercise that I call (tongue-ever-so-slightly-in-cheek) "Love It/Loathe It." Simply draw a line down the middle of the pages of a note pad, write Loved It at the top of one column and Loathed It at the top of the other, and then carry the pad around with you for a week. Any time you find yourself looking forward to an activity, or getting so involved in the activity that you lose track of time, or feeling invigorated when you're done with an activity, in the Loved It column scribble down precisely what you were doing. On the flip side, when you find yourself procrastinating an activity, or struggling to concentrate while you're doing an activity, or feeling drained and empty after finishing an activity, scribble it down in the Loathed It column. (In both cases, be sure to write down only activities that *you* are doing, not activities that are being done to you.)

This teasing-apart of your reactions to a regular week of your life won't take up much additional time, but it will force you to pay attention to the specific content of what you're filling your weeks with and how you're feeling about it. In short, it is the simplest way to gather the raw material you need to sharpen and refine your understanding of your strengths.

I have used my Creator-Stimulator combination to study human individuality, design strengths assessments, write books, speak on them, and build a company that trains managers to get better at getting the best from their people.

My sister is also a Creator-Stimulator. She used it to express her lyricism in ballet dancing. Then, after she retired and became a kindergarten teacher and hated it, she used it again to redirect her career back to the stage, where she could keep working with creative adults who wanted to learn how to perform as gracefully as she performs. She finished her masters in Fine Arts and now teaches at the London School of Contemporary Dance.

Michael didn't know his own strength and lost his way. Now, after fifteen years he is back at school, learning how to use his Teacher-Equalizer combination to design online software tutorials.

Lilia? Who knows? My hope, as her dad, is that she will take control of her genius, respect it, understand it, express it, and refine it, so that she can—in her own way and in a career of her own choosing—become one.

And you? Well, only you can decide.

CHAPTER 5

Strengths Assessment Technical Summary

Development and Validation

By Dr. Courtney R. McCashland

My StandOut Mission

We each have clear, vivid moments in time that shape every-thing that follows. Mine was at the age of twenty-one; I was a senior in college and filled with exuberance for life. I am the youngest of three, and my brother who was five years my senior was the truly gifted one. Brilliant, spirited, charming—he drew you in with his charisma. Yet sadly, he was always dissatisfied, searching for that euphoric freedom found when you invest your best and make something good happen. From my view, he wasted so much of what he was because he didn't choose to, or couldn't, find a way to engage his strengths.

Curt took his own life after only twenty-six turbulent years of living. I will never forget walking into the dimly lit room to find my father holding my brother's athletic, six-foot-long body in his arms. He rocked him back and forth and whispered, "Please, Lord, let us go back. Let us begin again." This image is forever with me.

In life we find ourselves cursed and blessed with things we can't control. Yet we have choices; and we have time. What we choose to do with our time is up to us. A witness to my brother's struggle and tragic death, I felt then, and feel to this day, tre-mendous accountability. Curt's death inspired my life's mission: to invest my own gifts to help others find theirs. My work with Marcus on StandOut is one expression of this lifelong mission.

Introduction

To fulfill this mission, Marcus and I turned to data and discovery from a decade of research with top performers, those who have consistently engaged their strengths for success. Our team of scientists and psychometricians reviewed patterns from more than a million talent assessments; analyzed hundreds of focus groups, interviews, and coaching sessions; and scrubbed survey results from hundreds of thousands of Strengths Engagement Track (SET) participants. The study of this robust data set over the years produced the content to formulate the nine strength Roles and the findings needed to measure them accurately.

This technical summary provides answers to questions you may have about the stability, reliability, and validity of StandOut.

The Research Approach

Between 2000 and 2010, we developed and administered a talent inventory to 435,564 participants in order to uncover the most reliable talents found to predict multi-industry job performance for six common job families—Leader, Manager, Professional, Sales, Service, and Support. During this period, more than two hundred focus groups and discovery interviews were administered as part of seventy-three validation studies designed to capture the profiles of top performers for each job family.

For the talents to be a valid predictor of success, we first had to ensure they were, statistically speaking, "reliable." Coefficient alpha is the most common statistical technique applied to assess the reliability of a unified construct measured by multiple items. Each talent was examined for internal consistency and analyzed using Chronbach's Alpha. Across the samples, alphas for the eighteen talents ranged from .64 to .93, demonstrating acceptably high internal consistency to the industry standard of alpha = .6. While the configuration and weighting of predictive talents varies by job family, Table 1 provides a summary of data from the eighteen talents most commonly found to have both high reliability and predictive validity across studies.

These eighteen talents are fundamental building blocks at the heart of the strength Roles measured by StandOut.

TABLE 1: RELIABILITY OF PREDICTIVE TALENTS BY STRENGTH ROLE			
Talent	Number of Items	Cronbach's Alpha Reliability Coefficient (n=94756)	Strength Role
Problem Solver	6	.76	ADVISOR
Common Sense	8	.69	ADVISOR
Initiator	6	.64	CONNECTOR
Team	9	.76	CONNECTOR
Adaptability	7	.76	CREATOR
Analytical	5	.76	CREATOR
Responsibility	8	.68	EQUALIZER
Structure	8	.79	EQUALIZER
Persistence	5	.69	INFLUENCER
Courage	7	.70	INFLUENCER
Achiever	5	.75	PIONEER
Belief	7	.68	PIONEER
Relator	8	.74	PROVIDER
Service	7	.84	PROVIDER
Positivity	5	.83	STIMULATOR
Intensity	5	.70	STIMULATOR
Developer	9	.76	TEACHER
Individualization	5	.77	TEACHER

To supplement patterns that emerged from this quantitative data set, we analyzed qualitative data from interviews with top performers and identified powerful talent combinations credited by the best as their secret to success.

The StandOut Instrument and the Sample

StandOut is an online assessment of talent—innate patterns of thought, feeling, and behavior—measuring nine powerful combinations called "Strength Roles." To measure which strength Roles are most dominant, we selected a test design and an item-type called "situational judgment." In the typical situational judgment test (SJT), you are provided with a variety of situations gleaned from critical incidents on the job. In recent years SJTs have increased in their popularity because of all item-types—from Lickert, to Binary, to Open-ended—they have shown the most power as a predictor of subsequent job performance. Research by McDaniel, Morgeson, Finnegan, Campion, and Braverman (2001) accumulated 102 validity coefficients and estimated the mean validity of SJTs to be .34, which as Weekley and Ployhart showed (2005), puts SJTs on a par with cognitive ability tests. In other research, Weekley and Jones (1999) found an SJT to provide incremental validity over cognitive ability and experience.

For StandOut, we designed situations from impact moments in life where a person's preexisting skills or technical knowledge would have minimal relevance to response options. We created hundreds of situations and talent-based response options, then trialed them in multiple test environments. Iterations of specific "StandOut" life situations and response options were reviewed to isolate distinct personality differences and subsequently tested in an alpha version of StandOut that was administered to 232,000 participants across jobs and industries globally in 2009–2010. The psychometric properties of the assessment were analyzed to refine StandOut's 146 situation and response combinations.

The 232,000 global participants who responded to the alpha version of StandOut had the option to report their demographic information. N = 6018 responded to at least one of the three demographic questions. Below is a summary of the demographic distributions.

TABLE 2: GENDER STATISTICS		
	Frequency	Percentage
Male	2568	50.1
Female	2561	49.9
Total	6018	

TABLE 3: AGE STATISTICS	
Statistics	Age
Minimum	17
Maximum	85
Mean	42
Std. Deviation	11

TABLE 4: EDUCATION STATISTICS		
Education Level	Frequency	Percentage
Less than high school	11	.2
High school graduate	169	2.8
Some college	636	10.6
Associate degree	227	3.8
Bachelor's degree	2188	36.4
Master's degree	1235	20.5
Postgraduate degree	445	7.4
Other	28	.5

The Scoring

In scoring the response options for StandOut, we measured each of the nine strength Roles twelve times across thirty-four situations. Thirty-two of the situations offered four response options. Two of the situations had weighted computations with all nine strength Roles measured in each. Not all of the response options presented for each scenario were scored in the overall calculations. The scores by strength Role were coded and converted into a t-score calculation to standardize the distribution. The calculations of the scores for each of the response options involved weighting for degree of difficulty for each scenario and dimension reliability for each strength Role.

StandOut Stability and Reliability

Would you expect your StandOut results to change if you take the assessment more than once? If you are curious, we can take a look at the stability and reliability of the assessment. An initial reliability measure of these scores was completed on a random sample of N = 269 participants from the US workforce using Chi-Square and test-retest analysis of mean Role levels. The sample of participants completed the assessment in October 2010 and then completed the same assessment again in May 2011. A statistical analysis called the chi-square test of independence was conducted, with a dichotomous variable labeled "Strength Role Match from Time One to Time Two."

In reviewing the top three strength Roles computed from the analysis, 90 percent of the sample had their leading Role in their top three from time one to time two, and 47 percent of the sample had two matches among their top three from time one to time two. All of the nine strength Roles had significant chi-square results, indicating that their presence in the top three roles on the initial administration of the assessment was significantly related ($p < .05$) to their presence in the top three roles during the second administration of the assessment.

TABLE 5: CHI-SQUARE TEST OF INDEPENDENCE RESULTS: N = 269		
Theme	Chi-Square	Significance
Advisor	5.039	.025
Connector	6.335	.012
Creator	11.245	.001
Equalizer	29.911	.000
Influencer	9.444	.002
Pioneer	25.460	.000
Provider	6.822	.009
Stimulator	28.906	.000
Teacher	20.530	.000

To scrutinize further the consistency of results from time one to time two, statisticians computed a t-test of change for each of the nine strength Roles. There were not significant differences in scores for any of the nine strength Roles from time one to time two ($p < .05$).

The Validity

The validity of an assessment must be evaluated with its intended purpose. The purpose of StandOut exists through its promise to help you pinpoint and channel your unique gifts. Built upon the principles of positive psychology, its application focuses your time on your strength Role as the path of least resistance to deliver results. Let's dig a little deeper into what StandOut measures, then take a look at how these strength Roles have been validated with top performing leaders, managers, and sales associates.

Content Validity: What the StandOut Strengths Assessment Measures. As we explored the data patterns from half a million talent assessments and listened through thousands of interviews to understand what explains success, it became apparent that the eighteen core predictive talents measured combine into common clusters with dominant peaks of frequency and intensity that best explain how someone will tend to think, feel, and behave.

StandOut measures how these talents converge into nine strength Roles, which are powerful, frequently reoccurring patterns that emerged through our research. For example, when you go looking for the answer to a question from my former head of research, you always learn something. While he knows the answer, he cannot just give you the answer. He needs to teach you how to find the answer on your own. He is a learner by nature and craves knowledge. He starts with where you are and develops you to be that much better. At his heart, in the language of StandOut, he is a Teacher. He peaks with intensity across three key talents—curiosity, individualization, and a coaching instinct—which come together to explain the brilliance of a Teacher. (Chapter 3 defines the nine StandOut strength Roles.)

Face Validity: Strengths Studies with Top Performers. In the study of top performers for a given job, you will find that specific talent clusters emerge to explain success. As part of our research in the validation of StandOut, we sought to understand excellence in practice through the lens of our nine strength

Roles. With each sample, we brought prior expectations from our experience. In every study, the stories through the data provided rich learning and strong face validity for StandOut.

The following bar graph provides a summary of composite results from a study of 140 top executives from a national financial institution. The average scores by strength Roles are ranked from the highest scoring Role to the lowest scoring Role. Given the regulated nature of the industry, and the inherent need of Equalizers to create balance and order through doing the right thing, we expected to find Equalizer as a the primary strength Role. And we did.

Top Executives at a National Financial Institution (N = 140)

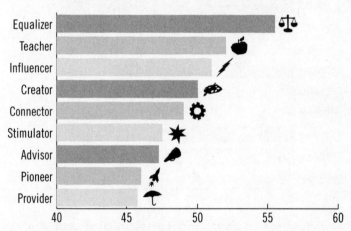

Likewise, aggregate data results from the study of fifty-five highest-rated general managers within a leading international hotel brand revealed three strengths at the top that would be expected given the demands of the job. First and foremost, an abundance of research would support that the best managers teach (Buckingham and Coffman, *First, Break All the Rules*, Simon & Schuster, 1999), so it is not surprising that their lead Role is Teacher—they understand the unique strengths of each team member and capitalize on those strengths to turn them into success. To do this, many create a spirited environment, where they honor and celebrate the success of each team member. This is the strengths path of Stimulators, which was ranked at three for the sample. Finally, to run a large hotel, it is critical to create order and structure—you need a clean room ready at the right time. So, it's not surprising the Equalizer is ranked number two.

Top General Managers of an International Hotel Organization (N = 55)

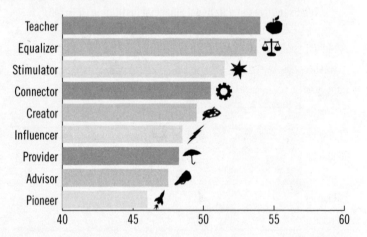

Forty-five sales organizations participated in a sales study of top talent. Each selected their two highest producers and invited them to participate in StandOut. A sample of N = 82 of the ninety selected as the best completed the assessment. You can probably predict what the aggregate data results revealed. Our anticipated strengths profile was validated with Influencer and

Connector at the top and Equalizer a close third. It's not surprising that the persuasion of the Influencer combined with their profound need to create a network—Connector—and make good on their commitments—Equalizer—merge to create the most successful sales representatives.

Top Sales Representatives from a National Association (N = 82)

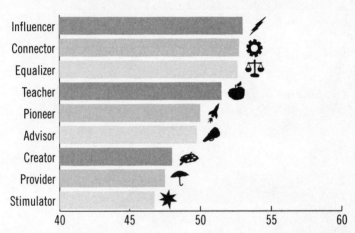

Face validity was also apparent across studies with engineers, teachers, humanitarians, and private school principals.

StandOut, by design, fulfills its promise to reveal accurately how your top talents intersect to define your strength Roles. The beauty is that each of us is truly unique. We each offer something of rare and significant value. This value is fully realized only when we take accountability to offer up our most dominant strengths as we serve in work, and in life.

A full technical report and summary is available at www. standout.tmbc.com.

Acknowledgments

I am blessed to share my life and work with strong personalities. Jane Buckingham, creative, insightful, and so very practical. Charlotte Jordan, who fights the "what is right?" vs 'what is best?' battle every day. Jaqai Mickelsen, who wanders through our training and development world wondering how he got here, determined to make it more fun, and more beautiful. This book, and the StandOut assessment at its heart, was begun as an attempt by me to understand them, and to pinpoint their greatest gifts. Thank you for your patience with me, and for sharing your gifts with the rest of us.

As you can imagine, a great deal has to happen for a book/assessment such as StandOut to emerge credible, complete and engaging. First, you have to design the assessment. Huge thanks here to my partner in psychometric crime, Dr. Courtney McCashland, whose experience was invaluable in crafting the scenarios, and who then wrote the technical summary which captures the statistical properties of StandOut.

Then you have to conduct all the interviews with excellent

leaders, managers, sales and service people, and derive from these interviews practical innovations and techniques. Tracy Hutton has been my calmly insightful partner in this ongoing research effort.

Then you have to design the assessment so that it appears at once substantial and friendly. Jaqai Mickelsen's creative strengths are on full display here—if you feel at home in the StandOut world, thank him. Alfonso Ramirez was his ace in the hole when it came to polishing the design elements to their shiny ruby best.

Then there's work you never see, the work that makes the whole thing work: the building of the relational databases, the programming of the algorithms, the testing, testing, testing. In the beginning there was Shaun Wanford, and now David Wagner toils behind the façade, providing us the structure and the certainty we need.

Then you have to write the book. Bryan Norman, my editor, has the kind of mind I aspire to have: penetrating, strong, gentle.

Then, when you are almost done, you give everything to Darren Raymond and say "Here. Fix it. Make it right." And instead he makes it better.

Thank you all.

Since we started TMBC in 2007 we have been blessed with some visionary partners who have expected more from us. Thank you for raising our sights: Gina Valenti and Phil Cordell of Hilton Worldwide; Telvin Jeffries, Nancy Blok-Anderson, and Amy Leschke-Kahle of Kohls; Lori Goler and Stuart Crabb of Facebook; Steve Stickel, Ben Putterman and John Lindner of Banana Republic; Camille Mirshokrai of Accenture.

We wouldn't have been able to reach these sights if it weren't for some extraordinary performers here at TMBC: Charlotte Jordan, who architects with such passion and precision all of the training we offer to world-class managers; Holly Dowling who infuses this training with her authority and her delighted spirit; Kristi Pavel, whose call everyone wants to take, and who we turn to for confidence; Maggie Hensle and Nancy Day-Blasberg, who bring our approach into people's lives, one intimate conversation at a time; Stephanie Daniels, who wins over everyone she meets, and who makes me look a great deal more responsive that I really am; Tiffany Criner, who somehow gets everyone to like her, and who then effortlessly transfers that goodwill to us; Elvie Moore, who smiles as the numbers balance, and who's still smiling when they don't; and Jessica Lee, who really runs the place.

Brian Hampton, thank you.

Mary Graham, thank you for your leadership.

Sheila Walsh, thank you for your awe-inspiring talent; and your generosity.

Jennifer Rudolf Walsh, thank you for your diamond spine; and your adoring heart.

Janie, Jack and Lilia, thank you for the material.

And all the love.

About Marcus Buckingham

Marcus Buckingham's groundbreaking ideas started a strengths revolution that has changed the business world. Beginning with *First, Break All the Rules* his books have sold more than 4 million copies. Through his training and development firm TMBC (www. TMBC.com) he teaches managers how to turn their associates' strengths into performance. Before launching TMBC, Marcus spent nearly two decades at the Gallup Organization studying what drives exceptional performance in the world's best managers. He has been profiled in the *Wall Street Journal*, the *New York Times*, *Fortune*, and *Fast Company*, and currently works with companies such as Facebook, Kohl's, Hilton, Microsoft, Chick-fil-A, Banana Republic, and the Walt Disney Company. A past member of the Secretary of State's Advisory Committee on Leadership and Management, Marcus graduated from Cambridge University with a master's degree in social and political science. He lives in Los Angeles with his wife, Jane, and their two children.

About Dr. Courtney McCashland

Dr. Courtney McCashland partnered with Marcus to design, develop, and validate the StandOut strengths assessment. As the president of the Global Assessment Division at Kenexa (www .kenexa.com) she leads Kenexa's mission to help companies find and develop the best individuals for every job. Kenexa is the exclusive global reseller of the StandOut strengths assessment. Over the last decade, Courtney has developed many cutting-edge assessments, including the Strengths Engagement Track (SET) for Marcus' best-selling book *Go Put Your Strengths to Work*, and the Survivor Profiler™ with Ben Sherwood for his bestseller *The Survivors Club: The Secrets and Science that Could Save Your Life*. Courtney was among a select cohort awarded scholarships from The Gallup Organization to attend the University of Southern California. She graduated first in her class with a doctorate in organizational leadership. She now lives in Lincoln, Nebraska, with her husband, Patrick, and their four children.